OECD Economic Surveys:
Norway
2012

This document and any map included herein are without prejudice to the status of or sovereignty over any territory, to the delimitation of international frontiers and boundaries and to the name of any territory, city or area.

Please cite this publication as:
OECD (2012), OECD Economic Surveys: Norway 2012, OECD Publishing.
http://dx.doi.org/10.1787/eco_surveys-nor-2012-en

ISBN 978-92-64-12724-1 (print)
ISBN 978-92-64-12725-8 (PDF)

Series: OECD Economic Surveys
ISSN 0376-6438 (print)
ISSN 1609-7513 (online)

OECD Economic Surveys: Norway
ISSN 1995-3321 (print)
ISSN 1999-0383 (online)

The statistical data for Israel are supplied by and under the responsibility of the relevant Israeli authorities. The use of such data by the OECD is without prejudice to the status of the Golan Heights, East Jerusalem and Israeli settlements in the West Bank under the terms of international law.

Photo credits: Cover © Shutterstock/Patrick Wang.

Corrigenda to OECD publications may be found on line at: *www.oecd.org/publishing/corrigenda*.
© OECD 2012

You can copy, download or print OECD content for your own use, and you can include excerpts from OECD publications, databases and multimedia products in your own documents, presentations, blogs, websites and teaching materials, provided that suitable acknowledgment of OECD as source and copyright owner is given. All requests for public or commercial use and translation rights should be submitted to *rights@oecd.org*. Requests for permission to photocopy portions of this material for public or commercial use shall be addressed directly to the Copyright Clearance Center (CCC) at *info@copyright.com* or the Centre français d'exploitation du droit de copie (CFC) at *contact@cfcopies.com*.

Table of contents

Executive summary 8

Key recommendations 9

Assessment and recommendations 11
    I. Macroeconomic policies to support sustainable growth 12
    II. Labour market policies 21
    III. Raising public spending efficiency 26
    IV. Reform of capital taxation 31
    Bibliography 37
    Annex A1. Taking stock of structural reforms 39

Chapter 1. **Value for money and public spending** 43
    Overall budgeting and expenditure planning 47
    Aiming at value for money 50
    Notes 64
    Bibliography 65

Chapter 2. **Tax reform in Norway: A focus on capital taxation** ... 67
    Main features of the dual income tax system 70
    The taxation of capital income and wealth 74
    Gift and inheritance taxation 83
    Corporate income taxation 85
    Local property taxation 90
    The stamp duty on property transactions 91
    The economic consequences of the recommended reform measures ... 92
    Notes 95
    Bibliography 95
    Annex 2.A1. Effective tax rates on savings in different asset classes ... 97

Boxes
    1. The Norwegian macroeconomic policy framework 13
    2. Summary of recommendations on macroeconomic policy 21
    3. Summary of recommendations on labour-market policy 25
    4. Summary of recommendations on value for money and public spending ... 31
    5. Summary of recommendations on the taxation of savings and wealth ... 37
    1.1. Recommendations on value for money in public spending ... 64
    2.1. Main characteristics of the Norwegian tax system 69
    2.2. Why the design of capital taxation matters for efficiency and growth ... 71
    2.3. Summary of recommendations on capital taxation 94

Tables

1.	Main macroeconomic and financial indicators	13
2.	Budget deficits 2001-12	14
3.	Budgeting for regional policy	28
4.	Effective tax rates on the real income from different assets	34
1.1.	Budgeting for regional policy	52
1.2.	Aspects of government regulatory oversight authority (2008)	60
2.1.	Tax revenue by main tax category, 2010	69
2.2.	Categories of capital taxation	73
2.3.	Tax treatment of asset classes	74
2.4.	Effective tax rates on the real income from different assets	75
2.5.	Marginal labour income tax rates	86
2.6.	Statutory tax rates for a Norwegian resident investing in Norwegian equity	87
2.7.	Statutory tax rates on the normal return of investing in Norway	89
2.8.	Use of the local property tax, 2010	90
2.9.	Budgetary and redistributive consequences of possible reform measures	93
2.A1.1.	Effective tax rates on the real income from different assets under alternative assumptions	99

Figures

1.	Gini coefficients before and after taxes and transfers	11
2.	Value of the Government Pension Fund Global	15
3.	Immigration, wages and unemployment	16
4.	Cyclical developments	17
5.	House prices and household debt in selected OECD countries	18
6.	Vulnerabilities in the Norwegian banking sector	19
7.	Employment in the private and public sector	22
8.	Labour force participation rates in 2010: an international comparison	23
9.	Population structure, 2010	24
10.	General government total outlays in 2010 or latest year available	26
11.	Household wealth and debt, second quarter 2009	33
12.	Revenue from gift and inheritance taxation, 2010	36
1.1.	General government expenditures as a percentage of GDP	44
1.2.	Production costs of public spending as a percentage of GDP, 2010	45
1.3.	Employment in general government and public corporations as percentage of the labour force	46
1.4.	Inter-municipality comparisons of social welfare indicators, 2009	55
1.5.	Ratio of aggregate tax administration costs per 100 units of net revenue collection	56
1.6.	Expenditure on general government outsourcing	57
1.7.	Increasing use of a regulatory oversight body at the central government level (1998, 2005 and 2008)	60
2.1.	Government tax receipts	68
2.2.	Average taxable gross financial capital per household, 2009	71
2.3.	Mainland revenue from capital taxation, 2008	73
2.4.	Household wealth and debt, second quarter 2009	76
2.5.	Valuation in the base of the wealth tax	79

2.6.	Total tax wedge on deferred consumption (for labour income earned in year 0)	80
2.7.	Recurrent taxes on net wealth, 2010	82
2.8.	Revenue from gift and inheritance taxation, 2010	84
2.9.	Non-oil business investment in international comparison	88
2.10.	Statutory corporate income tax rate, 2011	88

This Survey is published on the responsibility of the Economic and Development Review Committee of the OECD, which is charged with the examination of the economic situation of member countries.

The economic situation and policies of Norway were reviewed by the Committee on 12 January 2012. The draft report was then revised in the light of the discussions and given final approval as the agreed report of the whole Committee on 26 January 2012.

The Secretariat's draft report was prepared for the Committee by Paul O'Brien and Oliver Denk with statistical assistance from Josette Rabesona, under the supervision of Patrick Lenain.

The previous Survey of Norway was issued in March 2010.

This book has...

A service that delivers Excel® files from the printed page!

Look for the *StatLinks* at the bottom right-hand corner of the tables or graphs in this book. To download the matching Excel® spreadsheet, just type the link into your Internet browser, starting with the *http://dx.doi.org* prefix.
If you're reading the PDF e-book edition, and your PC is connected to the Internet, simply click on the link. You'll find *StatLinks* appearing in more OECD books.

BASIC STATISTICS OF NORWAY (2010)

THE LAND

Area (1 000 km²)		Major city regions (thousand inhabitants, 1.10.2011):	
Total	385.2	Oslo	1 251.9
Mainland	324.8	Bergen	387.3
Agriculture	10.1	Trondheim	259.0
Productive forest	80.0		

THE PEOPLE

Population (thousands, 1.10.2011)	4 973	Total labour force (thousands, 1.10.2011)	2 646
Number of inhabitants per km²	12.9	Civilian employment (thousands, 1.10.2011)	2 561
Net natural increase (thousands)	6.1	Civilian employment (% of total)	
Net migration (thousands)	13.9	Agriculture	2.4
		Industry and construction	19.4
		Services	78.3

PRODUCTION

Gross domestic product:		Gross fixed capital investment:	
NOK billion	2 523	% of GDP	19.8
Per head (USD PPPs)	57 231	Per head (USD PPPs)	11 319

THE GOVERNMENT

Public consumption (% of GDP)	22.0	Composition of Parliament (number of seats):	
General government (% of GDP):		Labour	64
Currrent and capital expenditure	45.6	Progressive	41
Current revenue	56.0	Conservative	30
		Socialist Left	11
		Centre	11
		Christian Democratic	10
Last general elections: September 2009		Liberal	2
		Total	169

FOREIGN TRADE

Exports of goods and services (% of GDP)	41.1	Imports of goods and services (% of GDP)	28.8
of which: Oil and gas	18.6		
Main goods exports (% of total)		Main goods imports (% of total)	
Food products and live animals	7.0	Food products and live animals	5.9
Finished goods	9.4	Finished goods	14.7
Machinery and transport equipment (excluding ships)	9.5	Machinery and transport equipment (excluding ships)	38.5
Mineral fuels	64.0	Chemical products	10.2
Goods exported by destination (% of total)		Goods imported by destination (% of total)	
Denmark and Sweden	10.2	Denmark and Sweden	20.3
Germany	11.3	Germany	12.3
United Kingdom	27.0	United Kingdom	5.9
United States	5.0	United States	5.4

THE CURRENCY

Monetary unit: Krone		December 2011:	
		NOK per USD	5.8910
		NOK per euro	7.7448

Executive summary

Norway continues to benefit from its well managed petroleum wealth and sound macroeconomic policies, achieving levels of well-being and social cohesion that have remained high by international standards. The strength of the economy and prudent supervision have helped the financial system to weather the financial crisis well, though high household debt and elevated house prices pose a risk. In the wake of the global slowdown and the euro area turmoil, the macroeconomic policy challenge has shifted towards preserving the momentum of growth in the context of the flexible inflation target and the well established fiscal framework. Public expenditure rose during the crisis and income redistribution remains extensive, in line with Norway's tradition. Ensuring that public spending is delivered in economically efficient ways remains a priority.

The **fiscal policy** stimulus was reined back a little in 2011 after the expansion in 2009-10. In 2012 the structural non-petroleum deficit, which is set to rise to just under 4% of the value of the Government Pension Fund Global, will have at most a small expansionary effect. There would be room within the fiscal guidelines to go for stronger expansion should economic activity turn out to be significantly weaker than projected. However, monetary policy should remain the first line of defence if the global outlook worsens, especially in the case of an intensification of the euro area crisis.

Monetary policy had begun to return to normality in the first half of 2011, as foreseen in the 2010 Economic Survey. Since then activity has slowed, international financial markets have again become turbulent, and annual consumer price inflation has remained well below the target of 2.5%. In these circumstances, the central bank was right to suspend the tightening cycle and then cut rates in December. It should resume tightening once there are risks of inflationary pressure, but there is also room for further easing in the event that economic conditions worsen.

Labour market performance is good overall with low unemployment and high participation. Average hours worked are low, due mainly to voluntary part-time work but also to high levels of sickness absence. The incidence of long-term sickness benefit and disability benefit to which it often leads may be reduced by measures taken in July 2011. Stronger steps to change incentives may well be needed. The recent private sector pension reforms need to be extended to the public sector.

Public expenditure occupies an important place in the economy, responding to Norwegians' desire for redistribution and a fair society through provision of public services. Careful attention to planning and efficiency is nonetheless required. An "efficiency unit" should be created to audit cost-benefit analyses and impact assessments carried out in spending ministries. A procedure for spending reviews, to assess the efficiency of major programmes and policies, should be established. Competitive outsourcing of the provision of public services to the private sector should be expanded where this improves cost-efficiency.

Norway's **tax system** achieves a high level of collection of receipts and revenue redistribution without overly undermining economic performance and while paying increasing attention to environmental externalities. The system is generally well structured with some innovative characteristics, but the taxation of capital still imposes distortions on savings. This is due to low taxation of residential property and uneven treatment of assets in the wealth tax, as theoretical calculations appear to show very high tax rates on some capital income. Greater tax neutrality could be achieved, equalising tax rates across different forms of capital income, while maintaining overall progressivity.

Key recommendations

Macroeconomic policies to support sustainable growth

1. Fiscal policy should continue to follow the longstanding guidelines. These allow for discretionary action to stabilise the economy if necessary.
2. Monetary policy should remain the first line of defence if the global outlook worsens, especially in the case of an intensification of the euro area crisis. There is room for further loosening if needed. Tightening should eventually resume if rising activity appears likely to bring annual consumer price inflation close to the target of 2.5%.
3. High household debt at floating interest rates and elevated house prices are vulnerabilities that macro-prudential policy and consumer protection should address. The strong financial supervision system should be maintained, including by ensuring that banks comply with higher capital requirements.

Participation in an inclusive labour market

4. Align the rules for early retirement in the public sector with those in the private sector.
5. Tighten access to the sickness and disability schemes, with stronger enforcement of back-to-work plans and independent checks on GPs' sickness and disability assessments.
6. If even tighter gate-keeping does not reduce take-up, reduce the replacement rate for long-term sickness and shift more of the costs onto employers.
7. Make the work assessment system for recipients of disability benefits more rigorous. Use the disability benefit system to help people into employment when possible.

Achieving high public spending efficiency

8. Increase the extent to which public expenditure and public administration and services are assessed on the basis of output indicators. Make greater and more consistent use of value-for-money analysis, with more transparent presentation of policy priorities.
9. Establish an "efficiency unit" with the power to audit cost-benefit and other assessment studies to ensure consistency across ministries.
10. Establish a system of independent spending reviews of specific public policy programmes.
11. Consider greater outsourcing of local and central government services to the private sector.

Reform of capital taxation

12. Improve capital taxation by aligning effective tax rates across assets. This should include reducing the implicit tax subsidy on owner-occupied housing, ideally by

introducing tax on imputed rental income or a national property tax, otherwise – though less desirable – by phasing out mortgage interest deductibility.

13. Investigate the impact of the wealth tax on effective tax rates, on tax avoidance and on incentives to invest. Phase out or reduce the wealth tax if the growth-redistribution trade-off is too unfavourable to growth.

14. Abolish stamp duty on real-estate transactions so as to promote mobility. Due to the possible effect on house prices, the timing should be considered carefully.

15. Replace existing allowances by a donor-independent lifetime allowance, so as to restrain avoidance in the taxation of inheritances and gifts.

Assessment and recommendations

Protected from the worst of the crisis by petroleum wealth and a sound macroeconomic policy framework, Norway continues to enjoy high levels of income and well-being

Norway's economy was protected from the worst of the recession induced by the 2008-09 financial crisis and should escape relatively unscathed from the current euro area turmoil. This resilience owes a lot to the improvement of the terms of trade and the prudent management of petroleum wealth, which has led to a very strong fiscal position. Norway scores high in international comparisons of material well-being, but also shows up well in other comparisons such as community, environment and safety, and overall life satisfaction. These high scores may be related to the Norwegian model of a relatively egalitarian society, where social consensus and a high degree of inclusiveness are important. Indeed, not only is wage inequality relatively narrow in Norway, but the amount

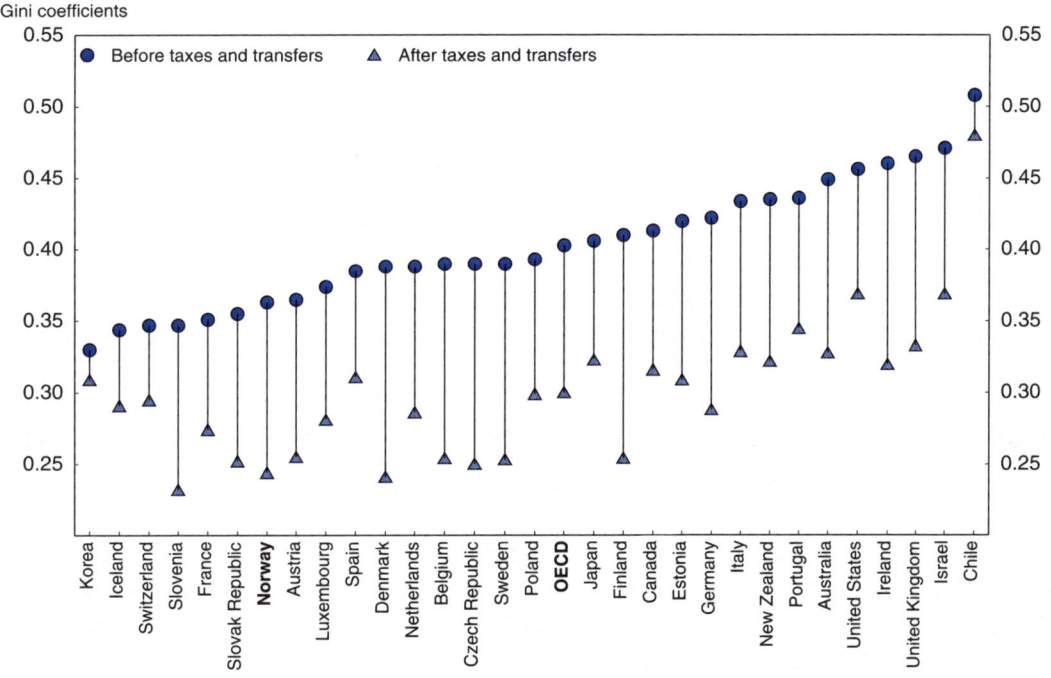

Figure 1. **Gini coefficients before and after taxes and transfers**
In the late 2000s

Source: Joumard et al. (2012).

StatLink http://dx.doi.org/10.1787/888932571969

of redistribution through the tax and benefit system is large, so that the distribution of net income is even more egalitarian (Figure 1). The generous provision of public services, such as education and health, also has a major role in offering all Norwegians an opportunity to realise their full potential. High public spending and associated taxation potentially imply significant efficiency costs, however, as they tend to distort economic incentives. This *Survey* discusses the overall management and control of public spending across the economy and focuses on certain aspects of the tax system.

I. Macroeconomic policies to support sustainable growth

The economy has been resilient despite the high level of uncertainty in the euro area

The mainland economy maintained some momentum well into 2011, especially in sectors closely connected to the petroleum industry or to public-sector service provision, but also in certain other dynamic sectors – such as financial intermediation, retail distribution, fishing, and fish farming. Signs of slowdown appeared in the second half of 2011 and the economy seems set to grow more slowly in the short term. Unemployment is nonetheless expected to remain low by historical and international standards. This enviable economic situation owes a lot to the rapid accumulation of petroleum wealth in the Government Pension Fund Global (GPFG) and the terms of trade, but also to supportive macroeconomic policies. Norges Bank, Norway's central bank, has conducted monetary policy consistent with both low inflation and low unemployment, with interest rates well below the "normal" rate of some 4-5%. Flexibility in the design of the fiscal framework has allowed a broadly neutral fiscal stance, with the structural non-oil budget deficit kept at about 5½ per cent of mainland GDP from 2009 to 2012, and at about 3¼ per cent of the value of the GPFG in 2011.

The effects of weakened confidence in the wake of the most recent global downturn are projected to restrain growth into 2012. The mainland economy should then regain momentum, and accelerate further in 2013 (Table 1). Norway has little trade exposure to troubled peripheral euro area countries, with its exports concentrated on relatively strong economies in Europe and, increasingly, Asia. Thus, the slowdown will be less pronounced than in many other OECD countries and the government, under current projections for the value of the GPFG, should keep the structural non-oil deficit somewhat below the level defined by the "4%" guideline. If, however, the financial turmoil worsens in the euro area and has negative global repercussions, the outcome could be much less favourable. In such a case monetary policy action should be taken, and if necessary the government could take discretionary fiscal measures to sustain demand, as foreseen under the macroeconomic framework (Box 1).

Fiscal policy continues to benefit from prudent management of petroleum revenues

Petroleum revenues continue to contribute to high national saving. Petroleum revenues are accumulated in the GPFG, which was worth over 160% of mainland GDP at the end of 2010, but rather less in late 2011 owing to equity market declines. A key contribution of the GPFG is to insulate the budget and the mainland economy from the immediate effect of swings in oil and gas prices, allowing the adjustment to take place over a longer period. The discretion allowed by the guidelines has some advantages, as the fluctuations in the value of the fund are increasingly due to financial markets rather than petroleum revenue, so the growth in the non-petroleum structural deficit as a share of mainland GDP has been quite rapid but not steady (Table 2).

Table 1. **Main macroeconomic and financial indicators**

	2008	2009	2010	2011	2012	2013
	Current prices NOK billion	Percentage changes, volume (2007 prices)				
Real GDP	2 510.9	−1.7	0.3	1.5	2.0	2.7
Private consumption	988.8	0.2	3.7	2.8	2.7	3.9
Government consumption	491.9	4.8	2.2	2.4	1.5	1.7
Gross fixed capital formation	548.0	−6.8	−7.4	6.0	5.0	4.8
Final domestic demand	2 028.7	−0.6	0.5	3.5	3.0	3.6
Stockbuilding[1]	7.0	−2.9	3.4	1.4	−0.8	0.0
Total domestic demand	2 035.7	−4.2	4.4	5.1	2.0	3.6
Exports of goods and services	1 218.0	−3.9	−1.7	−2.2	1.9	2.2
Imports of goods and services	742.8	−11.7	9.0	5.8	1.9	4.4
Net exports[1]	475.2	1.6	−3.2	−2.6	0.3	−0.3
Mainland GDP[2]	1 812.2	−1.8	2.1	2.6	2.7	3.6
Terms of trade		5.7	−4.2	−2.3	0.6	0.4
Consumer price index	−	2.2	2.4	1.5	1.9	1.8
Private consumption deflator	−	2.5	2.0	1.2	2.0	2.0
Unemployment rate	−	3.2	3.6	3.2	3.2	3.2
Household saving ratio[3]	−	7.3	7.4	8.7	8.5	7.7
General government financial balance[4]	−	10.7	10.6	12.5	11.5	10.7
General government gross debt[4]	−	49.1	49.7	56.5	51.3	48.6
Current account balance[4]	−	11.8	12.6	16.4	16.4	15.6
Value of GPFG, % mainland GDP[5]		150	166	160	172	
Structural non-petroleum budget balance, per cent of trend mainland GDP[5]		−5.4	−5.5	−5.3	−5.6	

Note: National accounts are based on official chain-linked data. This introduces a discrepancy in the identity between real demand components and GDP. For further details see OECD Economic Outlook Sources and Methods (www.oecd.org/eco/sources-and-methods).
1. Contributions to changes in real GDP (percentage of real GDP in previous year), actual amount in the first column.
2. GDP excluding petroleum and shipping.
3. As a percentage of disposable income.
4. As a percentage of GDP.
5. 2012 National Budget (October 2011). The estimated structural non-oil deficit in 2011 was revised down to 4.8 per cent of trend mainland GDP in the Final Budget Revision for 2011 (December 2011). Updated figures for 2012 will be published in the Revised National Budget in May 2012.

Source: OECD Economic Outlook, November 2011.

Box 1. **The Norwegian macroeconomic policy framework**

Fiscal policy works within a set of guidelines, agreed across all but one of the main political parties, on the use of revenue from oil and gas production. The current government augments these guidelines with self-imposed restrictions on tax changes.

The fiscal framework has two parts, a rule on the management of annual petroleum revenues and a rule on the management of the accumulated stock of revenue:

- All government revenues from oil and gas production, whether through taxation or ownership, less investment costs, are paid into the Government Pension Fund Global (GPFG). The GPFG invests exclusively in assets outside Norway.

- The so-called 4% rule stipulates that the central government deficit excluding petroleum revenues and adjusted for the cyclical position of the mainland economy should, over time, equal 4% of the value of the GPFG at the end of the year prior to the budget year.

> **Box 1. The Norwegian macroeconomic policy framework** (cont.)
>
> The figure of 4% was chosen because it was estimated that this was the long-run real rate of return the fund could expect. In this case, the rule amounts to preserving the real capital value of the GPFG. For the first decade or so, it achieved almost a 4% real return, but after stock market declines since the crisis and up to September 2011, the average return since the inception of the fund has been only 2.2%.
>
> A non-petroleum structural deficit equal to 4% of the GPFG is not a binding target for any particular year, the government is free to deviate from it in various circumstances, notably when discretionary fiscal action seems necessary to stabilise the economy, or when the value of the GPFG changes erratically. Although one of the aims of the GPFG is to preserve petroleum wealth for future generations, the guidelines do not explicitly require that cumulated deviations of the structural deficit from the 4% value should be zero. Use of the phrase "the 4% rule" or "4% guideline" in the text of this report encompasses both the 4% rule as outlined above and the underlying rule allocating all current petroleum revenue to the GPFG.
>
> The current government has operated since 2006 with a rule that any changes in the tax system should be calculated to be revenue neutral. If one tax is increased, another must be reduced to offset the estimated impact of the increase. In effect this should lead to a broadly constant share of mainland tax revenue in mainland GDP.
>
> **Monetary policy** is operated according to a flexible inflation target oriented toward low and stable inflation. The operational target is for consumer price inflation to be close to 2.5% over time. In aiming for this target, monetary policy is also to contribute to stabilising output and employment. The main policy instrument is the interest rate paid on banks' deposits in the central bank.

Table 2. **Budget deficits 2001-12**

	Central government structural non-petroleum deficit	
	As % of the GPFG	As % of mainland GDP
2001	5.5	1.8
2002	5.9	3.0
2003	7.1	3.4
2004	5.6	3.5
2005	4.9	3.4
2006	3.4	2.9
2007	2.7	2.8
2008	3.0	3.3
2009	4.4	5.4
2010	4.1	5.5
2011[1]	3.5	5.3
2012[2]	3.9	5.6

1. The estimated structural non-oil deficit in 2011 was revised down to 3.2% of the GPFG in the Final Budget Revision for 2011 (December 2011), corresponding to 4.8% of trend mainland GDP. Updated figures for 2012 will be published in the Revised National Budget in May 2012.
2. Projected.

Source: Ministry of Finance and *OECD Economic Outlook Database*.

The Ministry of Finance currently projects the value of the GPFG to increase from about 160% of mainland GDP at the end of 2011 to about 185% by 2025, assuming an oil price of NOK 427 (corresponding to about USD 72) per barrel (Figure 2). An oil price of

Figure 2. **Value of the Government Pension Fund Global**
As a percentage of mainland GDP

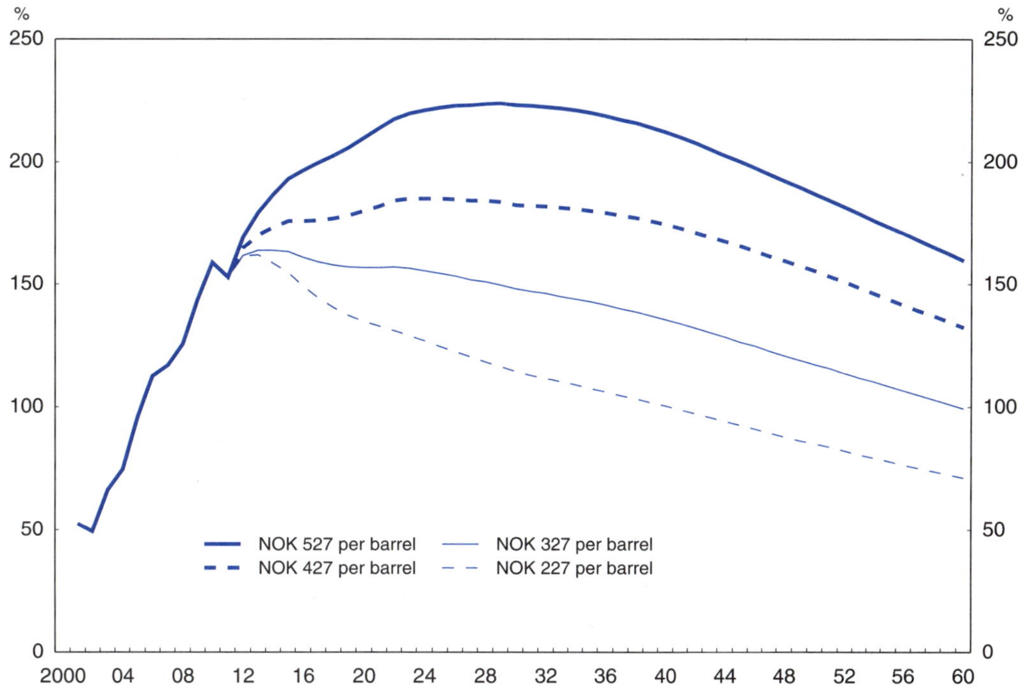

Source: Statistics Norway and Ministry of Finance.

StatLink ⟶ http://dx.doi.org/10.1787/888932571988

USD 85 per barrel would imply a higher fund value, around 220% of mainland GDP. On the central projection, the 4% rule would result in a non-oil structural deficit of 7% of mainland GDP in 2025. Though substantial, this would be insufficient to cover the potential longer-term gap in public finances due to higher age-related spending on pension and health. In addition, the annual real return on the assets of the GPFG between 1998 and late 2011 was only 2.2%, below the envisaged 4%. Although this is not a certain guide to future rates of return, together with the expected longer-term fiscal gap, it suggests that fiscal policy should aim at staying below the 4% path.

While the 4% rule dampens the "Dutch disease" effect, it cannot eliminate it altogether and the so-called traditional sector (non-oil traded goods) has been diminishing in importance. Despite this, it is important in setting wages. Rather than wages being determined by the relative bargaining strengths of different sectors, the general level of wage settlements is set by the social partners first considering the wage increase that the traditional sector can "afford". This tends to mean that in times of high demand pressure the acceleration of overall unit labour costs is attenuated. To some extent the pressure has, in recent years, been reflected instead in very high rates of net labour immigration (Figure 3).

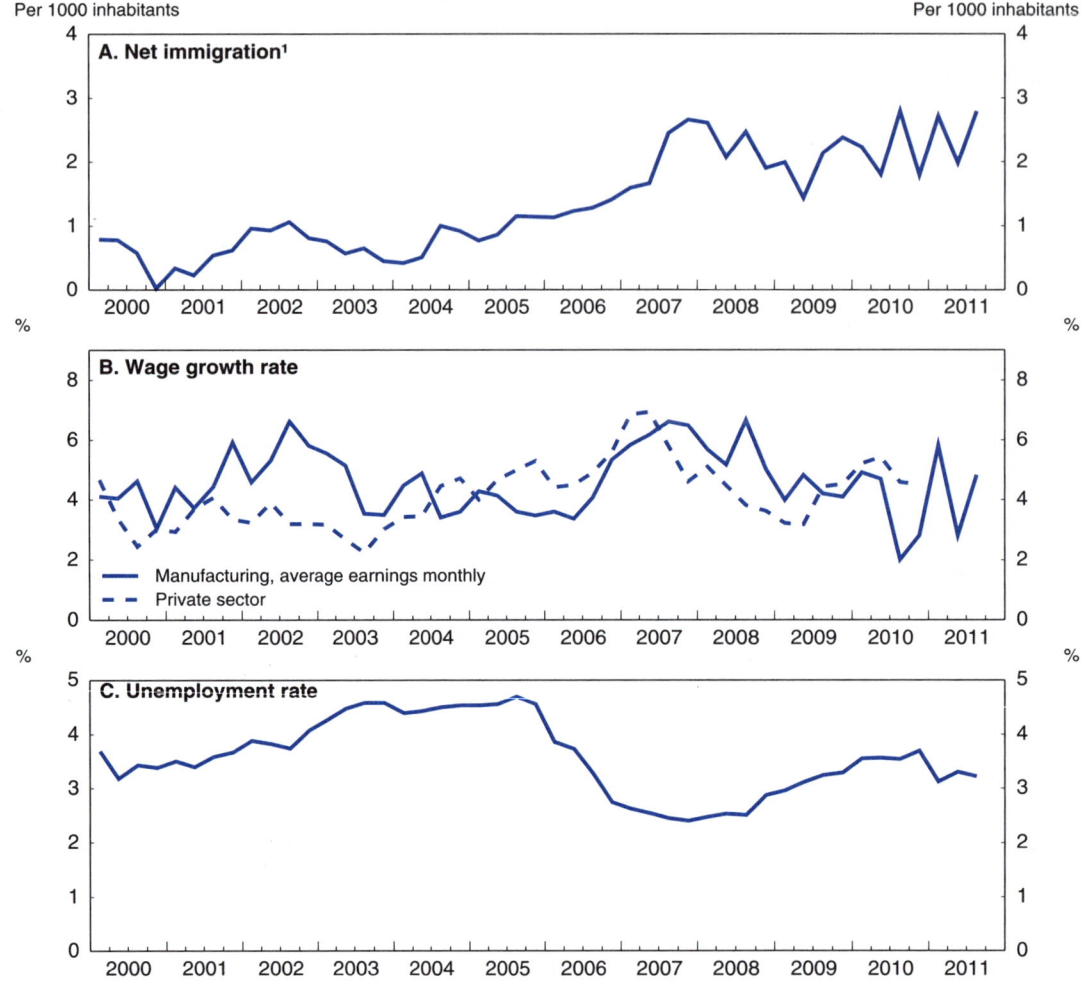

Figure 3. **Immigration, wages and unemployment**

1. Net immigration is total population inflow minus total population outflow.
Source: Statistics Norway and OECD Economic Outlook Database.

StatLink ⟶ http://dx.doi.org/10.1787/888932572007

Public accountability in fiscal policy

An increasing number of countries have recently set up independent fiscal councils to report on budgetary policy, as recommended by the OECD and others (Hagemann, 2010; Calmfors, 2010). As suggested in the 2010 Economic Survey, Norway has set up an Advisory Panel, which gives "expert judgment and advice" on modelling and long-term simulation issues, as well as on analyses reported to parliament in budget reports and the regular white papers on long-term perspectives. Two out of ten members are officials from the Ministry of Finance. The role of the panel should be kept under review, to see if its mandate could usefully be broadened in the future.

Monetary policy credibility allows interest rates to be kept low

Norway's flexible inflation targeting approach to monetary policy can present the authorities with a challenge, as domestic interest rates can have an uncertain effect on the exchange rate, depending on external factors – notably petroleum prices and interest rates in other countries. Although the annual consumer price inflation target of "close to 2½ per cent over time" has not always been met over the last 6 years, the shortfall has been mostly on the downward side, so expectations of low inflation are likely to be well-anchored (Figure 4). Keeping policy interest rates low, as the current uncertain situation requires, thus poses little risk to inflation. Low interest rates may have been encouraging the real-estate boom, which calls for a tightening of macro-prudential measures. Other indicators, such as banks' lending conditions and interest rates spreads, suggest that financial conditions are tighter than policy interest rates alone would suggest. In December 2011 the central bank lowered its key policy rate by 50 basis points to 1.75%, citing weaker prospects abroad, lower than expected domestic inflation and tightening conditions on financial markets. If the global and domestic economy turn out to be weaker

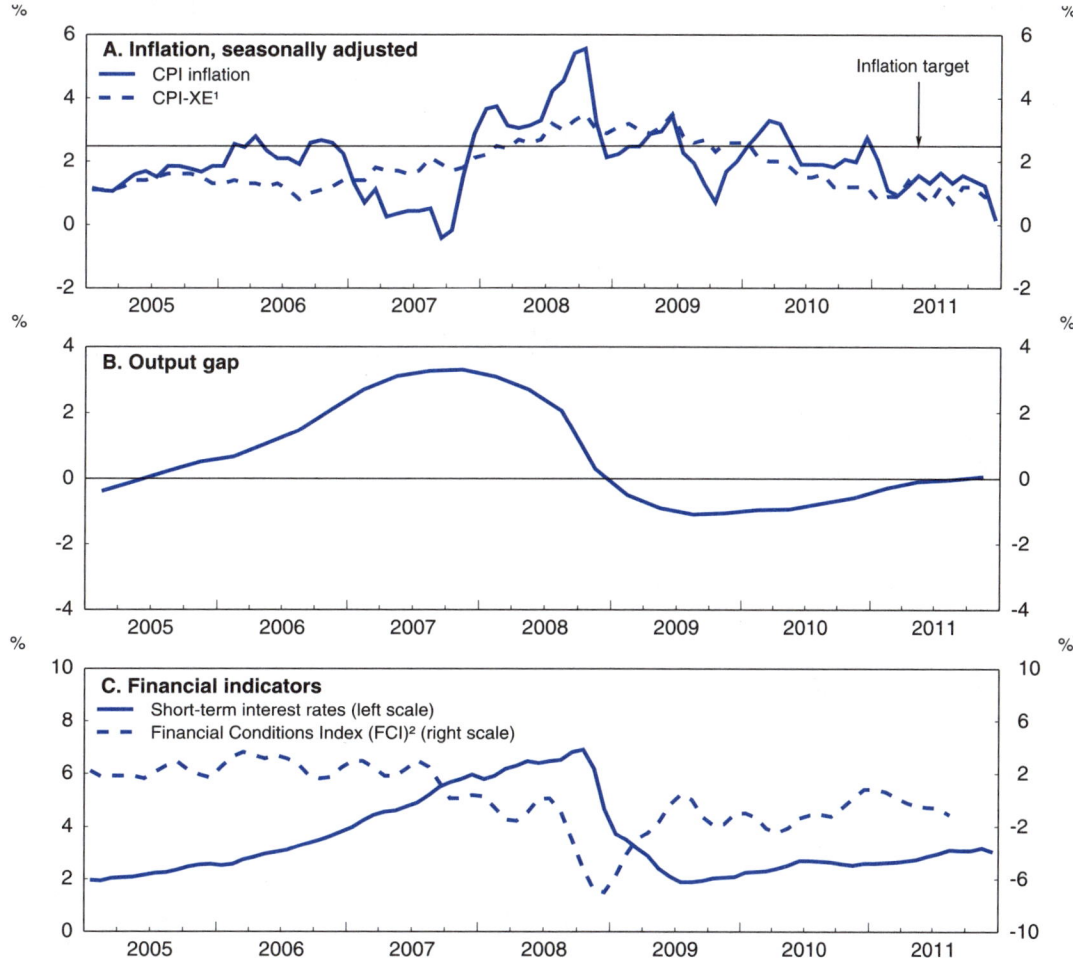

Figure 4. **Cyclical developments**

1. CPI-XE, calculated by Norges Bank, is the consumer price index adjusted for tax changes and excluding temporary fluctuations in energy prices.
2. Financial Conditions Index (FCI) includes 13 different indicators of financial conditions, such as share prices, credit supply and exchange rates (www.norges-bank.no/Upload/Publikasjoner/Staff%20Memo/2011/StaffMemo_0711.pdf).

Source: Statistics Norway and Norges Bank.

StatLink ⟶ http://dx.doi.org/10.1787/888932572026

than projected, the central bank should reduce the policy rate further and maintain it at a very low level for an extended period.

Real estate prices have continued to grow strongly

Property prices have renewed their upward path (Figure 5), growing at an annual rate of almost 10% for most of 2010 and into 2011. Credit to households has also been growing strongly, at around 6 to 7% a year, but this has been broadly matched by household income growth since 2007. Norges Bank has developed a tool to assess the resilience of the financial system, which considers internal vulnerabilities in the banking sector as well as external sources of risk (Figure 6). The greatest risks seem to stem from the household sector, reflecting historically high house prices and household debt, which is twice disposable income on average and almost exclusively at floating interest rates, an unusual situation in international comparison. In addition, the banking sector is subject to some funding risks which are primarily related to its significant reliance on foreign wholesale

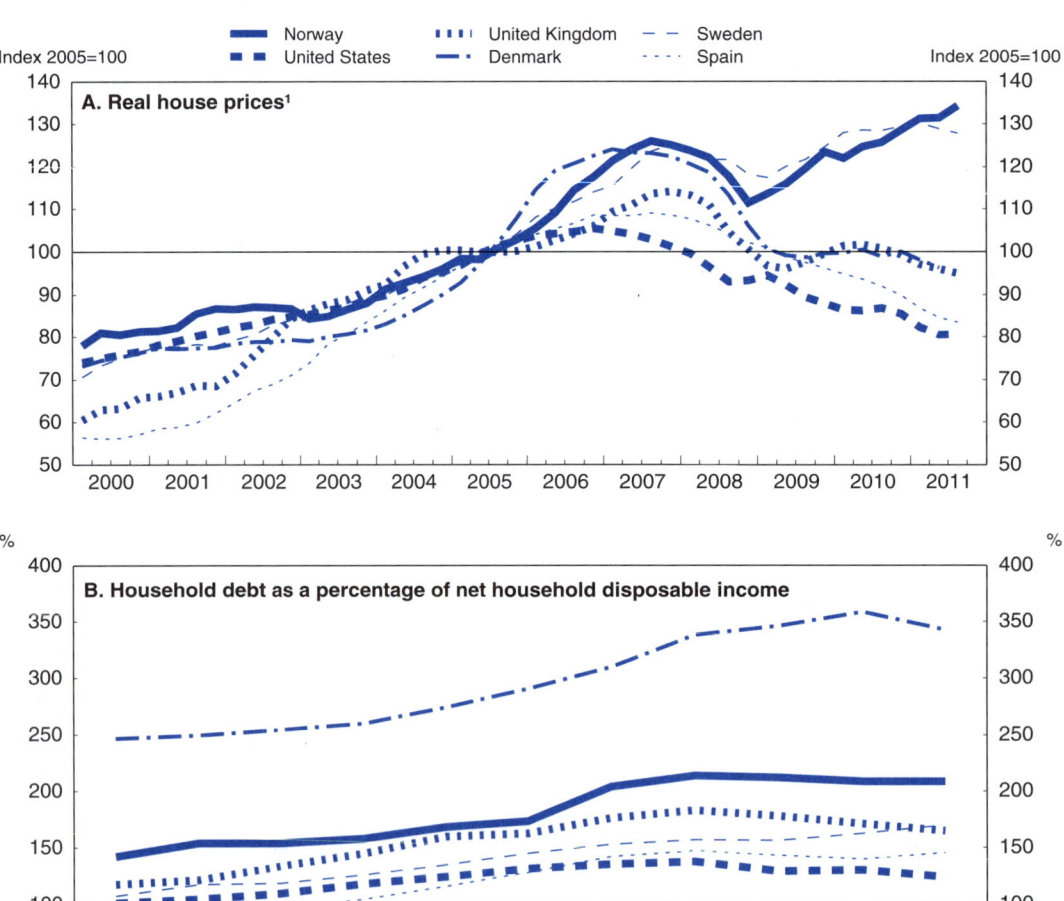

Figure 5. **House prices and household debt in selected OECD countries**

1. Deflated by private consumption prices.
Source: OECD Economic Outlook Database.

StatLink ⟶ http://dx.doi.org/10.1787/888932572045

Figure 6. **Vulnerabilities in the Norwegian banking sector**

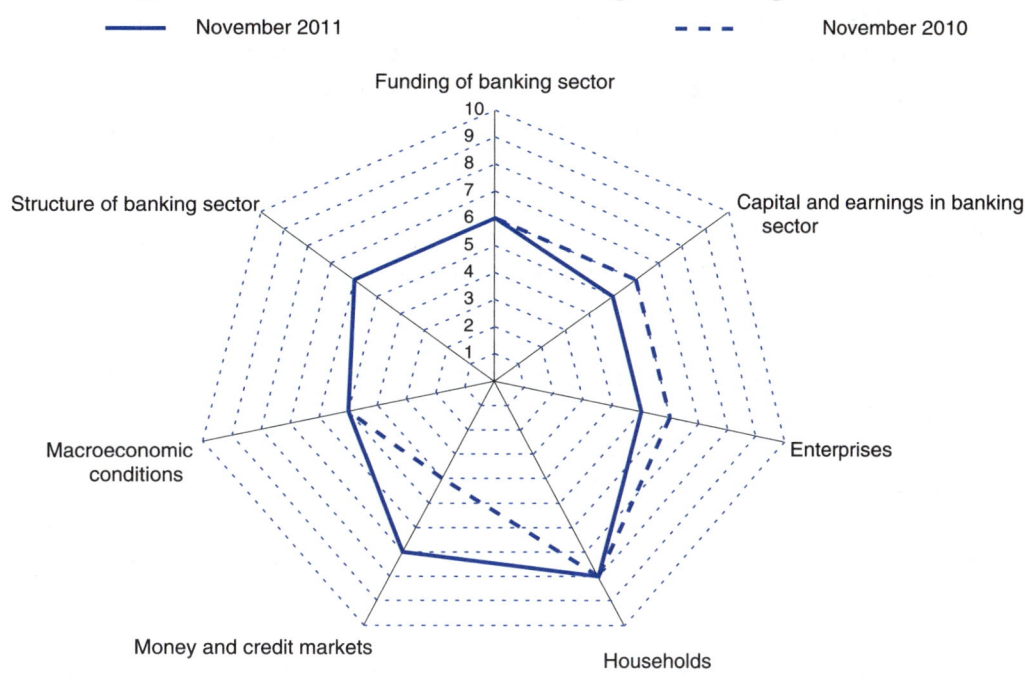

Note: A value of 0, i.e. the origin, denotes the lowest level of risk or vulnerability. A value of 10 denotes the highest level of risk or vulnerability.
Source: Norges Bank, Dahl et al. (2011).

StatLink ⟶ http://dx.doi.org/10.1787/888932572064

funds, while banks are little exposed to sovereign bonds in distressed euro area countries. Norges Bank's stress testing shows that banks' capitalisation would fall below required levels in a scenario where trading partner economies' suffer a downturn more severe than during the financial crisis of 2008-09, combined with a significant deterioration in international financial markets. These potential vulnerabilities of the banking system argue for maintaining high standards of financial supervision, in particular by ensuring that the banks are well capitalized with respect to the international Basel III norms and EU directives.

These potential vulnerabilities also suggest tighter macro-prudential policies are warranted. The authorities are constrained in regulating banks by EU rules and their application to EEA countries. Finanstilsynet (The Financial Supervisory Authority of Norway) advised banks in 2010 to apply stricter standards on mortgage loans where the loan-to-value ratio exceeded 90%. The guidance applies to both domestic banks and branches of foreign banks. Finanstilsynet tightened these guidelines in December 2011 due to continued high growth in house prices and household debt. The revised guidelines advise banks to lower the general loan-to-value ratio limit to 85% and to make allowance for a 5 percentage point increase in interest rates when assessing a loan applicants' debt-servicing ability. Finanstilsynet has stated that it may impose higher capital requirements if these guidelines are breached.

As in most countries, the low risk weights on mortgage lending encourage banks to expand in this market. Norway is also constrained because it cannot regulate Norwegian branches of foreign (mainly Nordic) banks, and stricter limits on domestic banks might cause many households to turn to branches of overseas banks, potentially inducing Norwegian subsidiaries of foreign banks (regulated in Norway) to turn themselves into branches (which would be regulated by the regulator of the parent bank). This could potentially leave much of the financial system outside the reach of the Norwegian regulator. Nordic co-operation on stricter capital requirements for housing loans would be a step in the right direction, but it is not clear what room Norway has to act on its own. There may be a further role for consumer protection legislation – which would apply to all borrowers and therefore to both banks and branches. Variable interest rate loans are the norm in Norway, and such borrowers are potentially very vulnerable to increases in interest rates. Such action could contribute to financial stability. Principles on financial consumer protection developed by the OECD were endorsed by the G20 heads of government in November 2011. They place particular emphasis on the need for financial consumer protection to be an integral part of the legal and regulatory framework. Financial service providers should provide clear information on possible risks, and financial education should be promoted. Norway is generally in line with international good practice in these areas, though improvements are needed in most countries.

In the Norwegian banking crisis of the early 1990s, bank losses on commercial property – rather than household mortgage debt – precipitated the crisis. Having fallen more sharply than housing prices in 2009, commercial property prices have bounced back more rapidly, growing at annual rates of 30% in 2011. Although growth in credit to companies has been low, the regulator should also continue to pay attention to banks' exposure to commercial property loans. Despite high property prices, the economy has been less unbalanced than some countries were in the pre-crisis boom: output of the construction sector remained between 4 and 4½ per cent of GDP for the last decade, though it did rise to close to 5% in the boom years.

While in some areas, such as the regulation of financial markets, progress has been made, in others the implementation of structural reforms recommended in past *Surveys* has been rather slow, in a few cases even backward (Annex A1). For example, since the last *Survey*, no significant measures have been taken to reduce tariffs and increase import quotas in the agriculture market. Similarly, no significant action has been taken to promote competition across a range of sectors, including the retail sector and postal services. Structural reforms should be implemented to address these weaknesses. In the labour markets, while the merger of the Public Employment Services and the National Insurance Services was completed, there is a need for increasing the flexibility in wage setting and a modernisation of the employment protection legislation. Other labour market reforms to promote job creation are discussed below.

> **Box 2. Summary of recommendations on macroeconomic policy**
>
> - Continue to manage fiscal policy within the established framework.
> - Aim to keep the structural non-oil deficit below the 4% rule, although there is room for discretionary action to sustain domestic demand in the event of a significant worsening of the euro area financial turmoil.
> - The stance of the central bank is appropriate. There is room for further loosening if needed. Tightening should eventually resume, once rising activity appears likely to bring annual consumer price inflation close to the target of 2.5%.
> - The good performance of the financial supervision system should be maintained, especially by ensuring that banks are well capitalized with respect to Basel III norms and EU directives.
> - The financial vulnerabilities resulting from high household indebtedness at floating interest rates may need to be addressed by further action on macro-prudential policy and consumer protection.

II. Labour market policies

Public sector employment helped to sustain the labour market through the recession

The labour market is characterised by low unemployment and high participation. Labour utilisation measured in terms of hours worked per working-age person is not high by international comparison, at least partly due to high levels of voluntary part-time working and sickness absence. High participation but short average working hours are probably a key contributor to Norway's high rating on subjective assessments of work-life balance. The dispersion of wages is also low; the ratio of the earnings of the highest decile of workers to that of the lowest is below that of all OECD countries except the other Scandinavian countries.

The fiscal expansion that was a response to the 2008-09 recession has been accompanied by increased public sector employment (Figure 7). This increase was small compared with the large increase in public sector employment that took place in the 1990s. It may be difficult to reverse because of the strong *de facto* security of employment in the public sector (although public sector labour contracts allow workers to be made redundant if the role defined in their job description is no longer needed). Over the past 20 years, public sector employment as a share of total employment in the mainland economy has been fairly stable.

The recent rise in local government employment has in fact been primarily due to higher employment in kindergartens and health and social services. The higher employment in kindergartens is partly accounted for by the newly introduced kindergarten promotion of the current government ("Kindergarten places for all children whose parents so wish"). About half of all kindergartens are privately run, not so much because of a policy choice by the local governments responsible but because they found it difficult to expand provision in the public sector in time to meet the objectives of the law. In other areas, the use of contracting out is more limited, but in many cases policy aims could be better served by wider use of contracting out to the private sector.

Participation rates are comparatively high in Norway, including quite a high share of part-time employment (Figure 8), while the employment rate was 77.5% in 2010, the third

Figure 7. **Employment in the private and public sector**
Seasonally adjusted

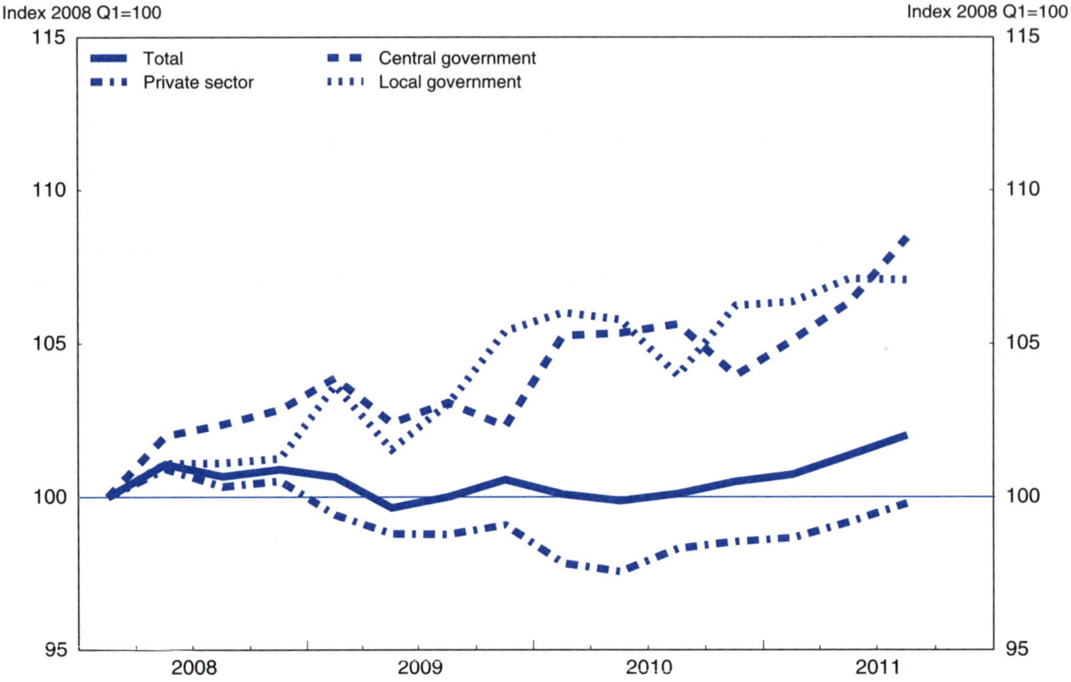

Source: Statistics Norway.

StatLink ⟶ http://dx.doi.org/10.1787/888932572083

highest among all OECD countries. Participation rates for the young, though still somewhat higher than elsewhere, fell in 2009 and 2010, seemingly as many chose higher education as an alternative to employment. Participation of older workers is also relatively high, despite high take-up of early retirement and disability pensions. It is likely to increase in the future following pension reforms which reduced the disincentive to continue working in the private sector, though strong disincentives still exist in the unreformed public sector scheme.

Norway's growing economy and high living standards attract large inflows of migrants, which are now 10% of the population. Despite high labour demand, employment rates for certain groups are relatively low, particularly among those with an Eastern European (outside the European Union), African, Asian and Latin American background (which together make up about half of all employed immigrants).

For unemployed immigrants as for many other unemployed individuals, Norway makes extensive use of active labour market programmes (ALMPs, such as public employment services, training schemes, employment subsidies). Experience in many countries suggests that not all forms of ALMPs are effective, and studies have shown this for Norway too (see *e.g.* Lorentzen and Dahl, 2006; and Rønsen and Skarohamar, 2009). The government should extend these studies to identify which ALMP programmes and which methods of delivery yield the best value for money, as well as to assess the relative efficiency of public and privately-run schemes. Resources should be concentrated on the most cost-effective methods.

Figure 8. **Labour force participation rates[1] in 2010: an international comparison**

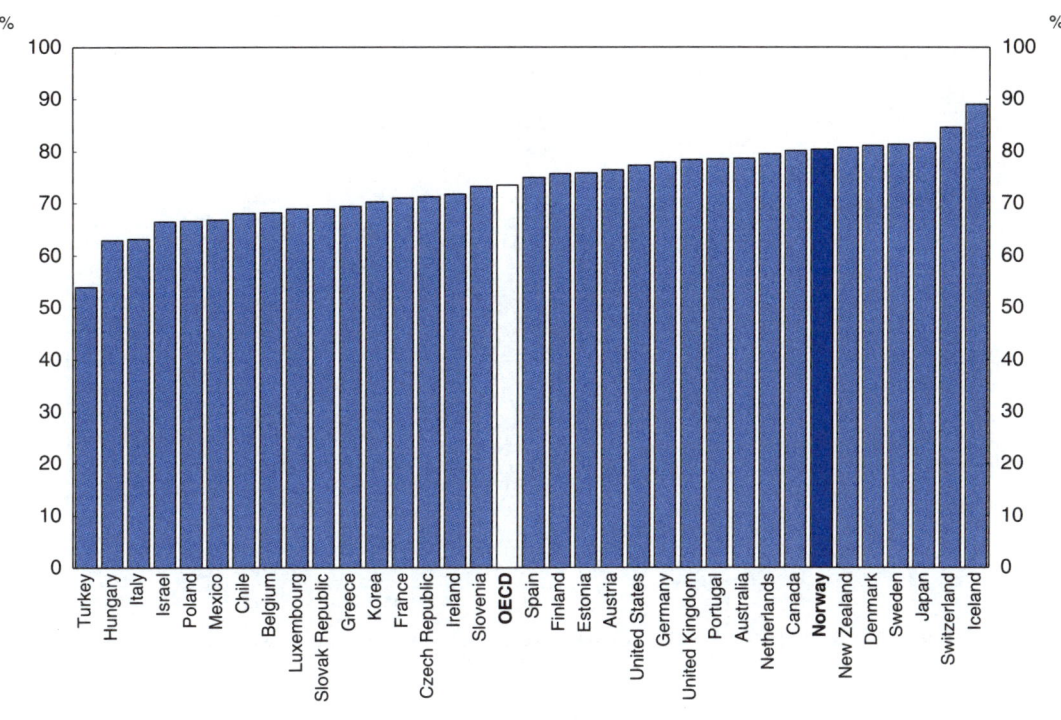

1. Women and men aged 15 and over.
Source: OECD, Labour Force Statistics Database.

StatLink http://dx.doi.org/10.1787/888932572102

Reforms in the sickness and disability schemes, and in public sector pensions, still fall short of what is needed

In the public-sector early-retirement schemes, people can receive an early-retirement pension at age 62, and from age 65 at the same level as if they retire later, creating a very high "implicit tax" on continued employment and a strong incentive to retire early. In the private sector, a similar scheme (AFP) used to operate but a recent reform, discussed in the 2010 *Economic Survey*, took effect for new pensioners from 2011. This reform has removed the strong disincentive to continue working, although the remaining subsidy due to partial state financing should be removed. Negotiations between public sector employers and unions should seek to reform the public sector scheme so as to fully align it with the principles of the reformed private sector system. It also is important to ensure that employees who transfer between the public and private schemes do not have their pension entitlements affected, so that the choice between public provision and contracting out of public services, discussed below, is neutral as far as workers' pension rights are concerned.

As discussed in previous *Economic Surveys* (in particular in 2005, 2007 and 2010) and the Disability Study (OECD, 2010b), Norway's high participation rates are undermined by its sickness and disability schemes. No other OECD country has such a high level of sickness absence and such a generous sickness benefit scheme (Figure 9). Around 5½ per cent of the employed are absent from work on a sick leave certificate. As a share of the population the number of employed-and-sick is fairly constant for those over 30 but, since the employment rate declines with age, the number of sick as a proportion of the employed

Figure 9. Population structure, 2010

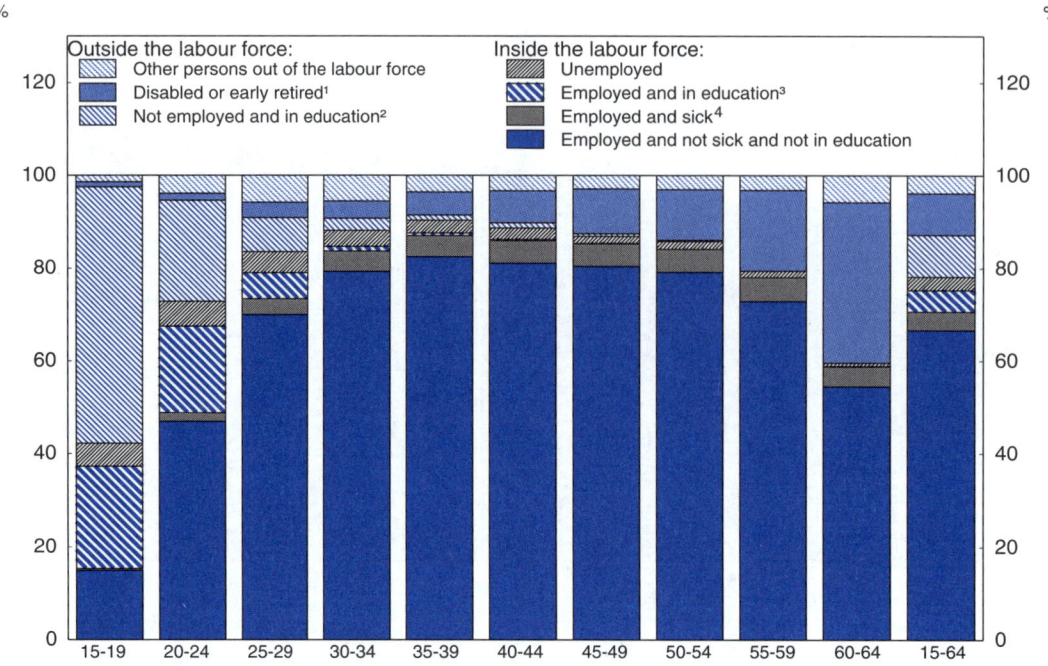

Note: This chart is based on a mixture of administrative data and survey data which may not be strictly comparable. "Employed and in education", "Not employed and in education", "Disabled or early retired" use self-reported data on main activity; according to Statistics Norway and Ministry of Finance, no factual data on the labour market status of persons in education and persons receiving disability or early retirement benefits are available.

1. This is an estimate based on the Labour Force Survey of the number of persons who are outside the labour force and self-report "Disability or early retirement" as their main activity. It is assumed that no person inside the labour force is disabled or early retired.
2. This is an estimate based on the Labour Force Survey of the number of persons who are outside the labour force and self-report "In education" as their main activity.
3. This is an estimate based on the Labour Force Survey of the number of persons who work part-time and self-report "In education" as their main activity. It is assumed that no such person is sick.
4. This is the number of employees who are on sick leave that is certified by a doctor.

Source: Statistics Norway.

StatLink ⟶ http://dx.doi.org/10.1787/888932572121

increases, reaching 8% for the 60-64 year-olds. Norway spends a higher share of GDP (4.8% in 2007) on sickness and disability programmes than any other OECD country and more than twice the OECD average of 1.9% (OECD, 2010b, Table 2.1). Sickness benefits are paid at 100% of the past wage for a whole year, for the initial 16 working days by the employer, then by the state. The scheme provides valuable insurance against a genuine long-lasting sickness, but it seems unlikely that genuine incapacitating sickness is so prevalent where other health indicators are good.

Governments have tried to improve gate-keeping, as documented in the 2010 *Economic Survey*, but the level of sickness absence remains very high. A further tightening was introduced in July 2011 in measures to provide for earlier and closer monitoring of sick leave, with provision for sanctions against the employee, employer and doctor for failure to follow up. Without strong sanctions and independent audits (which might be on a random selection basis) of doctors' assessments, there is a risk that this tightening will fail as in the past. The sanctions on employers and doctors who do not respect the tightened procedures should be strong. The new information system that allows doctors to benchmark their own diagnostic practices should be used to improve diagnosis, not to lead to a weakening of vigilance by those doctors who are currently relatively strict. Success in reducing unjustified sick leave would allow for an accompanying reduction in social security contributions. If the 2011 measures fail to cut entry into sickness benefit significantly, the government should introduce much stronger checks on doctors' assessments and/or increase work incentives by reducing replacement rates (as recommended in OECD, 2010b) to, say, 75-80% of the previous wage. A higher share of costs (beyond the current 16-day period) could also be shifted onto employers.

High levels of disability in Norway (9% of the population aged 15-64 receive a disability pension) also call for reform, linked with reform of sickness benefit, because many people on long-term sickness move onto disability benefits. As a fraction of GDP, expenditure on disability insurance in Norway is the highest across all OECD countries and the OECD indicator of disability compensation policy suggests that the Norwegian system is more generous overall than any other except that in Sweden (OECD, 2010b, Table 3.A2.1). To a considerable extent, disability benefit operates partly as a form of early retirement benefit – take-up rises strongly with age, but growing take-up among people under 35 (with a higher than average share of people assessed with a mentally-related disability) is an increasing problem.

A reform of the disability scheme was announced in mid-2011, to align the disability pension scheme with the reformed old-age pension scheme, but it did not address the existing problems of the high level of disability pension recipients. The government needs to provide clear guidelines to general practitioners in their role as gatekeepers to disability benefit, along the lines of the July 2011 measures for sickness benefit. But while sickness benefit is of limited duration, assignment to disability is effectively permanent, so gate-keeping must be even stronger. GPs' decisions should be subject to randomised but not infrequent checks. Those whose decisions reveal a strong bias towards leniency should have their authority to certify people for sickness or disability benefit withdrawn. In addition, the time on work assessment benefit (which covers the transition between sickness and disability schemes) must be better used to fit people for some work, and help to do more to facilitate the use of partial disability awards which act as income support while encouraging and, in part, enabling people to continue working; at the moment, more than 80% of disability benefit recipients receive full benefits.

> **Box 3. Summary of recommendations on labour-market policy**
>
> - Conduct credible statistical or other forms of testing to see which kinds of active labour market programmes give the best value for money and concentrate resources on these.
> - Fully align the rules for public sector pensions with the principles of the reformed system in the private sector, to avoid encouraging early withdrawal from the labour market.
> - Ensure the July 2011 revisions to guidelines on sickness benefit are fully implemented, with clear assessment guidelines to general practitioners and effective compliance monitoring. Extend a similar system to disability benefit and make more extensive use of partial disability benefit awards.
> - If access rates to sickness benefits do not fall significantly, further tighten gate-keeping, lower the replacement rate for long-term sickness absence and shift a greater part of the associated costs onto employers.

ASSESSMENT AND RECOMMENDATIONS

III. Raising public spending efficiency

Petroleum wealth allows high public expenditure

Norway's petroleum wealth provides the means to finance very high levels of public spending. The self-imposed restraint of the fiscal guidelines has been very effective in managing petroleum wealth and preventing too-rapid spending growth. Nevertheless spending has reached high levels and as a share of mainland GDP is the highest in the OECD (Figure 10). With such a large share of economic activity being influenced by public spending good mechanisms for ensuring money is spent wisely are important.

For example, there is evidence of overall inefficiency in the large compulsory education sector (see Economic Surveys of 2008 and 2010), and a number of areas of inefficiency in health spending (Economic Surveys of 2005 and 2010). Another example is regional policy, part of which is financed by the education, agriculture and public investment budgets, and thus cannot be easily evaluated. In addition to measures that can improve efficiency in specific areas, there is room to consider better ways to plan overall spending priorities, to assess policy efficiency and to ensure value for money in both small and large-scale spending decisions.

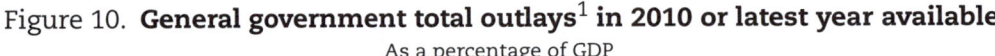

Figure 10. **General government total outlays[1] in 2010 or latest year available**

As a percentage of GDP

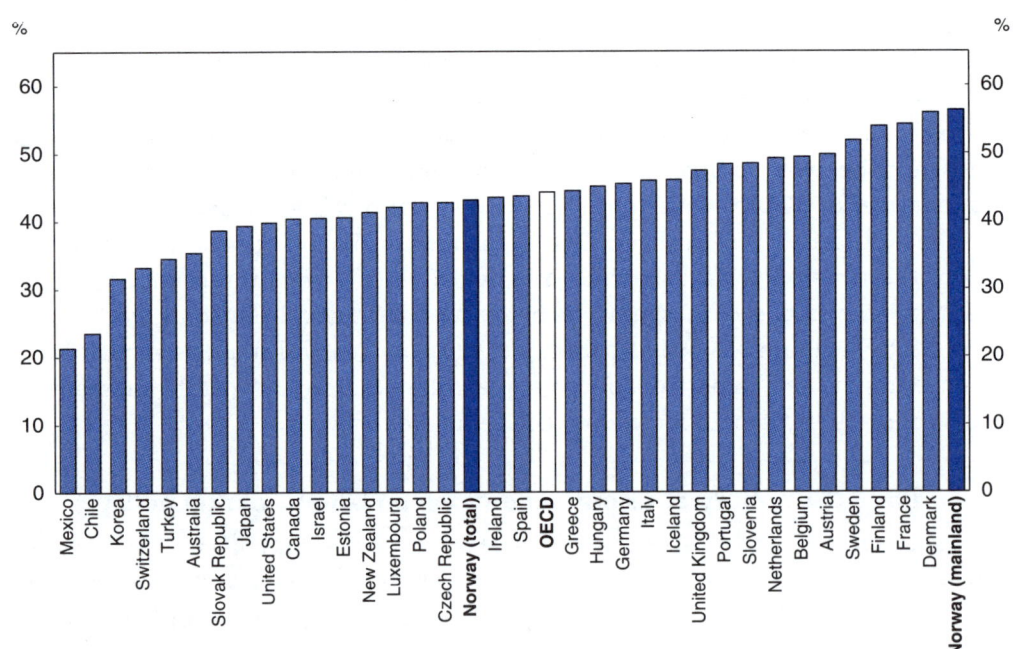

Note: Norway (total) divides total outlays by total GDP, and Norway (mainland) divides total outlays by mainland GDP. OECD area is the simple average of countries for which data are available (using Norway mainland). The figure for Ireland excludes the one-off impact of recapitalisation in the banking sector (EUR 31.575 billion in 2010).
1. Excluding interest payments.
Source: OECD, National Accounts and OECD Economic Outlook Database.

StatLink http://dx.doi.org/10.1787/888932572140

The budgetary planning horizon

Detailed spending allocations across ministries are carried out on a one-year cycle, as in most OECD countries, though there is also a revised budget in the spring that sometimes modifies allocations. Medium and long-term projections of spending by the Ministry of Finance are important tools for managing total spending. But, being based on the spending implications of existing policy settings, they may not be best suited for forward planning of policy changes, especially if they may involve switching spending between ministries. The one-year horizon at the central level contrasts with longer horizons elsewhere: transport spending is based on detailed 4-year rolling plans derived from a 10-year national transport strategy and local governments work on 4-year plans, for example.

While maintaining the one-year cycle of parliamentary debate and budget approval, a number of OECD countries have moved towards a longer period for planning expenditure, notably France, Italy, the Netherlands, Sweden and the United Kingdom. This is typically in the form of a multi-year plan (often 3 years) or framework that is rolled forward each year. In most cases a flexible form of multi-annual framework is used, in which the annual budget process can revise the whole framework. However, certain countries, including France, Sweden and the Netherlands (where significant proportions of spending are fixed for a full four-year period) have adopted a more fixed approach, in which the annual process adds an extra year but does not normally change the spending ceilings for years already planned.

Norway has considered multi-year budgeting in the past and rejected it. Some policymakers are concerned that such plans would set a floor on expenditure, with political pressure each year leading to upward creep. An implicit political commitment not to re-open the short-term debate each year would be necessary, leading to a better focus on efficiency and longer-term planning. Multi-year budgeting could facilitate planning within spending ministries, rather than achieve any particular level of spending, which is governed by the current fiscal guidelines. This need not jeopardise the existing system of effective control of total spending and the fiscal stance. The current fiscal framework enjoys strong political support and its key elements must be conserved, but a re-examination of the pros and cons of multi-year budgeting may be timely.

Monitoring of public expenditure "output" has improved

Norwegian public expenditure management has been moving for several years towards an output-based system where the allocation of resources is tied to policy objectives, thereby allowing policy makers and expenditure managers to compare performance across different areas. In local government, the relevant information system – known as KOSTRA – seems effective, as municipalities can compare their own spending patterns with those of others; at least some municipalities are doing this actively. The corresponding information system for central government functions is not yet being effectively used in this way, perhaps because a clear definition of output in many functions is more difficult.

In some cases information that is already available, or could be made available, may not be being used as effectively as it could be. In education, previous *Economic Surveys* noted the under-performance of the education system given the amount of resources devoted to it (OECD, 2008; Boarini, 2009); the latest (2009) PISA results show some improvement, with performance generally slightly above the OECD average, but still not commensurate with the well above-average level of resource-use. There are legitimate worries about using test results to improve performance, for example excessive testing, teaching to tests, taking proper account of students' backgrounds. But effective accountability requires better use of such information. In Oslo, such performance information is used to some extent to reward school principals and teachers, suggesting that it can be useful. Earlier OECD recommendations that the Ministry of Education at least conduct a comparative study to see whether the Oslo experience could be used more widely have not yet been followed up. Nevertheless, policy has moved towards improving teacher qualifications, focusing more on core competencies in maths and reading/writing, in line with OECD recommendations in these areas.

Regional policy is popular, but output is hard to measure, although its cost is becoming easier to identify

Regional subsidies command a high degree of popular support in Norway and may provide public goods, for example by reducing congestion in larger cities. But this support may be partly because the costs are not explicit. The main explicit instrument is social insurance charges which are lower than the standard rate, even zero, in the most remote areas, but almost every spending department in Norway has extra costs associated with the difficulties of providing public services to a geographically low density population. To a considerable extent the low density is actively encouraged by deliberate policy to lower the cost of living in certain areas.

Some improvement in transparency is, however, apparent in the budgetary treatment of regional policy. The cost of social insurance reductions is some NOK 11 billion or about ½ per cent of GDP. Furthermore, a table in the 2011 budget documentation shows that a number of other measures address regional policy objectives, although many are classified under agriculture or fisheries policy. Together with the social insurance measures, identified budgetary measures add up to over 1% of GDP (Table 3). The information in the

Table 3. **Budgeting for regional policy**

Item	2011 budget allocation or estimated implicit cost	
	NOK billion	% mainland GDP
Budget figure for the cost of regional policy	34.4	1.7
of which:		
Reduced social contributions		
Private sector	7.0	0.4
Public sector	5.2	0.3
Reduced income tax and other measures for Finnmark and North Troms	1.2	0.1
Reduced tax on energy, district and other grants in northern Norway	3.9	0.2
Direct subsidies to agriculture	11.5	0.6
Transport and other infrastructure subsidies	2.6	0.1
Public services, environment	2.2	0.1
Capital costs of road and other infrastructure investment	n.a.	n.a.
Other implicit costs:[1]		
Subsidies to agriculture via Producer Support Estimate	4.5	0.3
Education	2.0	0.1
Total	40.9	2.1

1. Implicit costs are based on illustrative assumptions: half the market price support component of the PSE for agriculture; one fifth of the possible gains from increasing school size in education.
Source: Ministry of Local Government and Regional Development and OECD estimates; see Chapter 1, Table 1.1.

budget documentation covers only current expenditure, and no corresponding figures are presented for investment spending.

Although helpful, the information now published is incomplete. Some implicit costs, admittedly rather hard to evaluate, such as those of keeping larger numbers of small schools or maintaining and building roads, are missing, as well as the non-budgetary costs of agricultural policy. The latter, measured by the Producer Support Estimate (PSE) calculated by the OECD, could reasonably be understood as partially motivated by regional policy for agricultural support and are large. As Table 3 shows, when estimates of the implicit cost of these items are included, the total resources devoted to broadly-defined regional policy may be over 2% of GDP, equivalent to around one third of the education budget, and a multiple of the cost of the labour cost subsidies, the main explicit policy instrument.

An array of good public expenditure assessment tools could be used more coherently

Such aggregate information can be used as part of an assessment of overall spending priorities, while at a more detailed level cost-benefit analysis (CBA) is an important tool. More consistent use of CBA is needed, and some paradoxes need addressing. It is fairly easy, for example, to find the guidelines for CBA of road projects (though not for rail projects) on ministry websites, but not the analyses themselves. Indeed, almost no road projects that are actually implemented show an *ex ante* excess of benefit over cost. This is not necessarily inconsistent with good use of CBA. Benefits that cannot be quantified in monetary terms can legitimately be sufficient to justify carrying out such a project, and research has shown that some components of CBA or impact assessments do influence Norwegian decision makers' priorities. However, when decisions are taken that overrule the conclusions of CBA or other impact assessment procedures, the responsible ministry should make clear the grounds on which such decisions are made. This is useful both on grounds of transparency but also to develop consistent practices in the face of particular but recurring circumstances.

Other systems for ensuring that public spending is used in a cost-efficient way also exist in Norway, notably a "quality assurance system" for large public projects. In this system evaluation is carried out by outside consultants rather than within the public administration, ensuring a degree of independence. Procedures are quite long and thorough, requiring an initial investigation of at least two alternative ways of meeting a project's objectives as well as an analysis of the relative costs and benefits of doing nothing. This independence is illustrated by the fact that the system has recently called into question a major public investment in a carbon capture and storage scheme, to which the government had attached high priority. The investment has been postponed. The cancellation of a bid for the Winter Olympic Games is another example. The National Audit Office, which reports to parliament but has a large degree of independence, can also investigate spending efficiency, but (in common with parliamentary audit offices generally) it is largely constrained to judge policy against the objectives set by parliament. Finally, guidelines for Regulatory Impact Assessment (RIA) have been in place for some time, but according to the Ministry for Government Administration, Reform and Church Affairs they are not consistently followed in some ministries, despite the existence of a new panel established to ensure better use of RIA. The Budget Department in the Ministry of Finance monitors whether ministries spend money according to plans, and examines new policy initiatives, but has only a limited role in assessing value for money in ministries' implementation of agreed policies.

Ensuring that CBA is applied consistently across all projects and ministries should be a priority. A commission on the revision of the CBA guidelines is due to report in 2012. One way to get more coherent use of value for money tools would be to assign responsibility, with strong political backing, to an "efficiency unit" which would monitor analysis and decision making in all ministries and report publicly where required procedures are not followed effectively. To contain costs, this oversight should take the form of random but in-depth checks of CBA (and RIA and other assessments) rather than systematic monitoring of all of them. The efficiency unit could be under the responsibility of the Ministry for Government Administration or the Ministry of Finance. Once in place, additional force could be given to the unit by the Audit Office, which could, under its own mandate, report on whether the efficiency unit was effectively improving compliance with assessment guidelines and, if not, insist on better enforcement.

In order to redirect expenditure over time to more cost-effective areas, a system of "efficiency dividends" could be envisaged. Under such a system, all ministries would have their budgetary allocations reduced by, say, 1% each year. The resulting "pool" would be allocated across ministries according to priorities decided by the government as a whole.

An additional measure would be to set up a spending review system that could take major policy areas one at a time and conduct in-depth reviews of policy aims and effectiveness. Investigating panels should have independent chairpersons and could use both experts from ministries and outside experts, including from other countries, with a remit both to assess existing policies and to propose modifications that would meet policy objectives more cost-effectively. One of the purposes of such a system would be to provide background information for the multi-annual spending framework discussed earlier, as it does in the United Kingdom, for example.

Private sector involvement in delivering public services through contracting out via competitive tenders can help to improve efficiency in public expenditure. Local government in particular has done this on some occasions. The recent rapid expansion in kindergarten provision, following a change in the law, was achieved largely through private provision. Private provision is almost non-existent in the rest of the education system, however. Under the new approach to output-based budgeting, project managers, even in central government, are in principle free to choose whether to use public or private sector providers to meet their targets but little use is made of this possibility. Public-Private Partnerships (PPPs), favoured in some OECD countries, are little used in Norway. They can be misused, for example if they serve mainly to by-pass ceilings on public expenditure by substituting private funds, and the government may not be well-placed to assess some of the risks involved. The benefits of private sector expertise in management and cost-reduction are achievable through outsourcing with the careful definition of contractual terms. The financing side of all projects should remain fully accounted for in public budgets. Guidelines on PPPs are currently being discussed by the OECD's Public Management Committee.

However, as mentioned earlier, since 2008 employment in the public sector has been rising even while private sector employment has declined. Although public sector employees can legally be made redundant if their job disappears, in practice this rise in public sector employment cannot easily be reversed. Many government functions are close to policy-making and require specialised knowledge, long-term accountability and confidentiality. These are good reasons for excluding the possibility of private sector involvement. But encouraging the consideration of its use in other areas, especially for simple service delivery, while meeting at least as good standards as public sector providers, could give efficiency gains that release public resources for other uses.

> **Box 4. Summary of recommendations on value for money and public spending**
>
> - Establish a procedure for independent "spending reviews" – evidence-based assessment of specific policies or programmes – as a counterpart to internal assessment. A unit to support them could be located in the Ministry of Finance but the chair should be independent and with the power to recruit key outside experts.
> - Further increase the extent to which expenditure is assessed on the basis of output indicators.
> - Explore the possibility for greater use of private sector out-sourcing in provision of local and central government services.
> - For cross-cutting issues, especially regional policy, place more emphasis on publishing estimates of overall spending, including implicit spending through methods such as market price support and cross-subsidisation, and assessing this overall spending against policy objectives.
> - Explore the possibility for greater use of performance-based information and incentives for public sector workers to increase efficiency.
> - Ensure that the implementation of Regulatory and Environmental Impact Assessment, cost-benefit analysis and other policy assessment tools is consistent across ministries. Establish an "efficiency" unit, with the responsibility of auditing the use of these tools to ensure this consistency, publishing its reports. Such a unit should be subject to performance auditing by the National Audit Office.
> - Consider the introduction of an "efficiency dividend" system in which mandatory across-the-board cuts in ministerial budgetary allocations are redistributed annually to priority areas.
> - Require a reasoned justification for decisions which do not respect the conclusions of cost-benefit analyses or impact assessments.
> - Assess the pros and cons of adopting multi-year budgeting, for example in which spending ceilings for the main spending lines in each ministry are fixed for the next three years, consistent with expected returns on the GPFG and other revenues.

IV. Reform of capital taxation

Progressive, broadly-based labour income taxation is a feature of Norway's dual income tax system

Norway's egalitarian income distribution and high level of social cohesion is achieved not only through low wage inequality (see Figure 1), but also through significant redistribution of income through the benefit system (*i.e.* cash transfers) and public expenditure (*i.e.* transfers in kind). In addition, some reduction in income inequality can also be attributed to the overall progressivity of the tax system. Since in aggregate labour income far exceeds capital income, the bigger contribution to income redistribution within the tax system is through labour income. The current design of the tax system ensures that it raises a lot of revenue, and it generally does so without harming incentives disproportionately, as is evidenced by strong economic performance. Norway has pioneered a number of new instruments in environmental taxation whose level is one of the highest in the OECD area. Furthermore corporate income taxation represents an unusually large component of tax revenue reflecting the large amounts of tax payments from petroleum companies.

Like Denmark, Finland and Sweden, Norway has a dual income tax system which treats the taxation of capital income separately from the taxation of labour income. Capital income is taxed at a low proportional rate, while labour income is taxed at progressive rates. This approach seeks to limit the type of distortion induced by the traditional comprehensive income tax system, which taxes capital and labour in the same way and results in double taxation of earned labour income and high tax rates on real returns. The dual approach was however not perfect, and Norway had to make adjustments to its initial system in reaction to personal business owners evading taxation by reporting labour income as capital income and incorporating solely for tax purposes. These loopholes were successfully closed in a reform in 2006. This introduced the innovative concept of a rate of return allowance that raised the statutory tax rate on capital income above the "normal" (or risk-free) return to that on labour income but did not increase the taxation of the normal return. This way, the reform decreased the scope for the type of tax avoidance that reduced the progressivity of the tax system, while limiting the negative effects on investment incentives.

Taxation of savings and wealth pursues many aims, often ineffectively

Some problems remain, however. Taxation varies widely across asset classes. Ministry of Finance calculations suggest that taxation of real returns can be over 100% for fixed-income assets and equity shares and as low as 0% for owner-occupied housing. This is likely to result in significant distortions to saving and investment behaviour and also to affect income distribution. The harsh tax treatment of interest on bank deposits, through the taxation of purely inflationary gains, especially affects households at the lower end of the income distribution for whom this type of savings instrument is likely to be relatively important. The high taxation of equity income, caused by insufficient inflation adjustment of depreciation allowances and cumulative taxation of capital incomes through the wealth tax, may lower economic growth. The extraordinary tax advantages to housing investment are likely to influence the way in which households hold their overall wealth, favouring residential investment at the expense of more productive categories of investment (Figure 11). They also raise the vulnerability of the financial system to macroeconomic shocks. House prices have risen to new historic highs and household debt is also high (see Figure 5). The government should design a package to reform the taxation of capital that, when accounting for purely inflationary gains and the wealth tax, would align a household's capital income tax rates across all asset classes at a level close to its labour income tax rate.

The current system taxes savings and wealth in many forms: through the personal income tax (on interest, rents, dividends and capital gains) and the corporate income tax; through the wealth tax and the local property tax; and through the stamp duty on property transactions and the gift and inheritance tax. The wealth tax is due at a rate of 1.1% on

Figure 11. **Household wealth and debt, second quarter 2009**

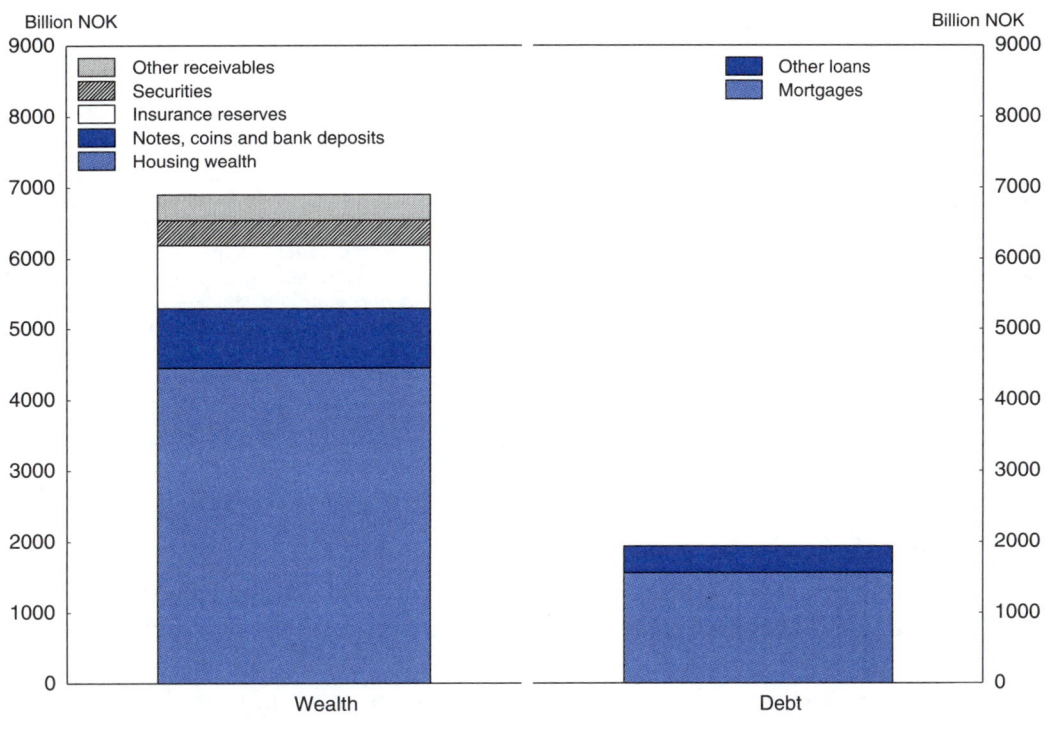

Source: Statistics Norway and Norges Bank.

StatLink http://dx.doi.org/10.1787/888932572159

assessed wealth in excess of NOK 750 000 and is currently paid by 17% of the adult population.

To illustrate the effective tax on each asset class, an overall tax rate (subsuming personal income tax, corporate income tax and the wealth tax) applying to each asset can be calculated. Table 4 presents effective tax rate (ETR) calculations by the Ministry of Finance. The ETR is defined as the percentage reduction in the annual real rate of return caused by the tax system and is shown for four investment classes: interest-bearing accounts, shares, owner-occupied housing and rental housing. The calculations are done for a nominal rate of return of 4% and an inflation rate of 2%. These approximate the nominal rate of return to government bonds and consumer price inflation in Norway since 2000; a similar pattern emerges for different choice of these values. The left column applies to citizens who do not pay the wealth tax, the one on the right to those who do.

The table illustrates the wide variation in tax rates across asset classes and the high ETR, well above that on labour income, on the capital income of wealth tax payers unless there are ways to avoid these taxes. The statutory capital income tax rate is 28%. Since this is applied to the nominal return, the ETR – when the nominal rate of return is twice the inflation rate – amounts to 56% (or twice 28%). For people not paying the wealth tax, the income from interest-bearing accounts, shares and rental housing is taxed in full, while nothing is due on owner-occupied properties. The discrepancies are even more pronounced for people paying the wealth tax. Since owner-occupied housing and rental housing are given reductions in the base of the wealth tax, interest-bearing accounts and

Table 4. **Effective tax rates on the real income from different assets**

	Without wealth tax (%)	With wealth tax (%)
Interest-bearing accounts	56	113
Shares	56	113
Owner-occupied housing	0	14
Rental housing	56	79

Note: The calculations are done for a nominal rate of return of 4% and an inflation rate of 2%, which correspond closely to the nominal rate of return to government bonds and consumer price inflation in Norway since 2000. The effective tax rates (ETRs) apply to an extra NOK of saving by a Norwegian resident investing in a Norwegian asset. The ETRs for shares are based on nominal depreciation rates which are a reasonable approximation to how the Norwegian tax system functions as tax depreciation depends on the cost price (not the repurchase price) and the expected life span of the asset. The ETRs for owner-occupied housing and rental housing are independent of the degree of debt finance *versus* self-finance when assuming that mortgage interest rates equal savings interest rates. See Chapter 2.
Source: Ministry of Finance.

shares are taxed 8 times as much as owner-occupied housing and 1.5 times as much as rental housing.

Re-alignment of effective tax rates is feasible

ETRs should be aligned across all asset classes to reduce distortions in the allocation of savings and capital. Taxation of owner-occupied housing would be put on the same basis as for other capital by re-introducing the taxation of imputed rents and capital gains at the current statutory capital income tax rate of 28%, while retaining the deductibility of mortgage interest and other expenses. Such a reform would need to be phased in gradually to alleviate the economic impact on current owners who would experience windfall losses as a result. In most regions, the rental market would be sufficiently large to enable reliable estimation of the unobserved rents to owner occupation. Elsewhere, house prices and average price/rent ratios could be used as an indirect means to derive the imputed rents. An alternative to taxing imputed rent would be a national tax on the market value of owner-occupied property, which would be quite similar. Either of these reforms would be largely pointless unless the tax base were regularly revalued, so a strong political commitment would be necessary. Taxing owner occupation would also eliminate the current tax discrimination against the less well-off who tend to rent and hence on whom a significant fraction of the tax due on rental housing is likely shifted.

Given the political and practical difficulties of taxing imputed rents or property values experienced in many OECD countries, an alternative – though less desirable – option is to phase out mortgage interest relief. It would raise the ETR on the debt-financed part of owner-occupied housing towards those on other asset classes, while leaving the returns to the self-financed part untaxed. However, because of the difficulties ring-fencing interest related to mortgages on owner-occupied houses, an abolition of mortgage interest relief would probably introduce some debt shifting in the personal income tax and thereby undermine the uniform treatment of different sources of capital income.

Taxing the imputed rents and capital gains from owner occupation would align tax rates across asset classes under the capital income tax, but would not remove the distortions due to the current undervaluation of owner-occupied housing, rental housing and business property in the base of the wealth tax. To remove this distortion to capital allocation, the base of the wealth tax should include all assets at full value. However, if this were done, at current tax rates the theoretical ETR for people paying the wealth tax would rise to 113% for all asset classes. These very high ETRs could be reduced either through the capital income tax or the wealth tax. However, any significant reduction in the capital income tax rate would reduce the tax rates on above-normal returns below the one on labour income, providing individuals with incentives to declare labour as capital income. It would also bring capital income taxes on the personal and corporate level out of line. It would therefore have to involve a rather substantial reform of the entire tax system.

Norway's wealth tax raises little revenue, but imposes very high marginal effective tax rates on capital income

The revenue from the wealth tax is small, only about 0.2% of all household wealth or around 0.8% of mainland GDP. Evidence suggests that wealth taxation is subject to avoidance and evasion behaviour. The cumulation of the capital income tax and the wealth tax, which both effectively tax the same base, results in ETRs of above 100%. Such a high rate should be a strong disincentive to investment and indeed the ratio of mainland investment to GDP is relatively low. The fact that investment nevertheless continues suggests that there are ways to avoid one or more of the taxes, that many wealth tax payers have a strong desire to build up their wealth even though this does not increase their lifetime consumption, or that investment is increasingly undertaken by foreigners (who are not subject to the wealth tax), or maybe that taxpayers are not aware of the ETR. Given the potential long-run consequences of penalising saving and investment, the Norwegian authorities should investigate this issue.

Rather few countries in the OECD levy a wealth tax. Sweden abolished its wealth tax in 2007, to avoid cumulative taxation and because, as in Norway, it suffered from exceptions that created loopholes and encouraged tax planning. The wealth tax is controversial in Norway and has been much in the public debate. This controversy is reflected by the leader of the Confederation of Trade Unions (LO), the main workers' organisation in Norway, arguing for an evaluation of the wealth tax, on the ground that it hinders investment. Phasing out the wealth tax would reduce the ETR on all assets (if imputed rents and capital gains on housing were taxed) to 56% in Table 4, close to the top marginal tax rate on labour income (including social security contributions) of 54%. However, phasing out the wealth tax might be politically difficult because of its association with redistribution. A less complete reform should at least remove the undervaluation of housing and business property, while at the same time lowering the 1.1% statutory rate of the wealth tax. Raising the current threshold of NOK 750 000 would reduce the number of people paying the wealth tax, but not solve the underlying problem of high marginal effective tax rates.

If the wealth tax were removed, the ETR on interest-bearing accounts and shares would be 56%. This is above the top marginal tax rate on labour income and considerably higher than the lowest rate. Small savers would thus pay a higher rate on income from their savings than on their labour income, while richer people would pay roughly similar rates. To reduce this effect, the government could introduce a personal allowance on capital income of a certain amount per year (say, NOK 10 000) for each citizen. Variants of such an allowance are in place in several OECD countries, such as Germany. Such an allowance would enable households to transfer some of their labour income to later in life without incurring taxes on the income earned. An ETR of 0% (up to the allowance) would particularly benefit poorer households for whom bank deposits (which currently attract an ETR of 56%) are likely the most important type of investment. Since for rich households the

ETR would be unchanged at the margin, the allowance would strengthen the overall progressivity of the tax system, counterbalancing some of the effects from phasing out the wealth tax. There is, however, a risk that such an allowance would inflate over time due to lobbying activity and also set a precedent which might lead to public demands for allowances elsewhere in the system.

The tax base of the gift and inheritance tax should be broadened

In Norway, gift and inheritance taxation generates little revenue. Generous annual and lifetime allowances provide the wealthy with many tax avoidance possibilities, thus undermining redistribution policy. Gifts to a taxpayer's children are taxed to avoid erosion of the inheritance tax base. By contrast, gifts to others remain untaxed, while children's inheritances are tax-advantaged. Farms, non-listed shares and partnerships enjoy preferential rules. To broaden the base of the gift and inheritance tax, current allowances and preferential rules could be replaced with a single allowance for each individual that applies to the total lifetime amount of taxable gifts and inheritances received from all donors. Currently, the revenue from gift and inheritance taxation is small (Figure 12), less than half the revenue from the stamp duty on property transactions. For its part, the stamp duty distorts the allocation of residential property and reduces residential and labour mobility. It should thus be phased out over time – due to the possible effect on house prices, the timing should be considered carefully.

Figure 12. **Revenue from gift and inheritance taxation, 2010**[1]

As a percentage of GDP

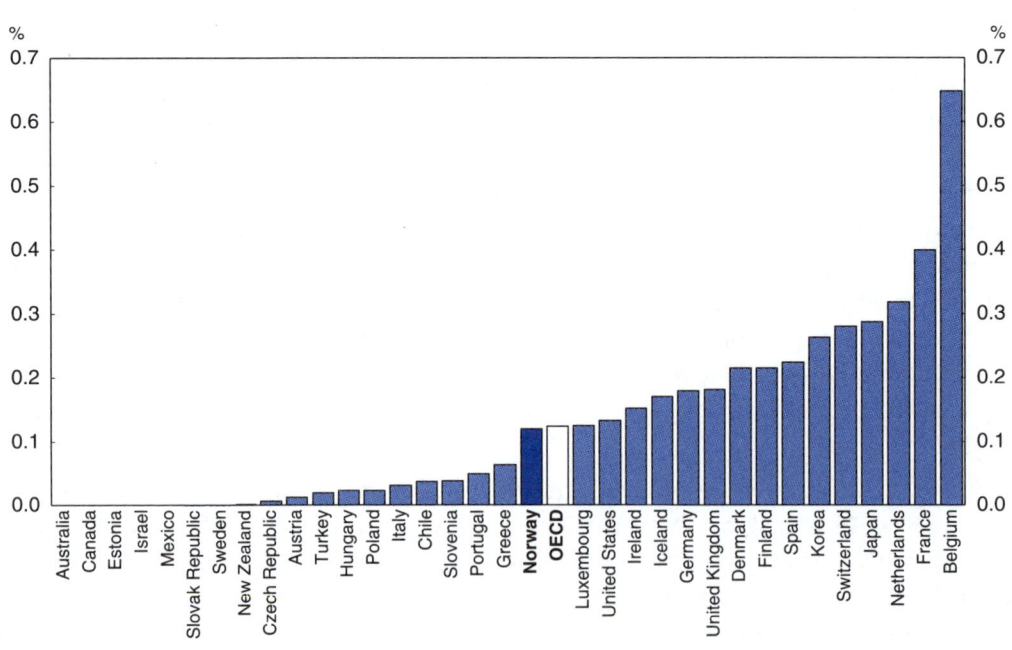

Note: Data from Norway refer to mainland. OECD area is the simple average of OECD countries for which data are available. The figures of GDP used for the calculations are those of the latest update available.
1. Or latest year available.
Source: OECD, Revenue Statistics Database and National Accounts Database.

StatLink http://dx.doi.org/10.1787/888932572178

Tax reform should promote growth through improvements to the allocation of capital and work and investment incentives. It could be designed to be broadly neutral with respect to revenue and income redistribution. Subjecting owner occupation to taxation and increasing gift and inheritance taxation would offset revenue losses from the proposed annual allowance on capital income and abolition of the stamp duty as well as from possible reductions in the wealth tax. The introduction of the taxation of owner-occupied housing, the annual allowance on capital income and the increase in gift and inheritance taxation would reinforce redistribution through the tax system, while reducing the wealth tax and stamp duty would have opposite effects.

> **Box 5. Summary of recommendations on the taxation of savings and wealth**
>
> - Align the taxation of different asset classes.
> - For housing this should include reducing the implicit tax subsidy of owner-occupied housing and removing the special treatment of real estate in the wealth tax.
> - Ideally, imputed rents and capital gains from owner-occupied property should be taxed at the same rate as other capital income. An alternative would be a national tax on the market value of owner-occupied property. A third possibility would be to eliminate mortgage interest deductibility on owner-occupied property, although this would still leave distortions in place.
> - To promote mobility, abolish stamp duty on property transactions. Due to the possible effect on house prices, the timing should be considered carefully.
> - To restrain avoidance by the wealthy in the taxation of inheritances and gifts, replace all existing allowances and preferential rules with a donor-independent lifetime allowance.
> - Investigate the impact of the combination of wealth and capital income taxes on effective tax rates, on tax avoidance and on incentives to save and invest. If the growth-redistribution trade-off is too unfavourable to growth, phase out or reduce the wealth tax. If the wealth tax is phased out, consider introducing a personal allowance on capital income.

Bibliography

Boarini, R. (2009), "Making the most of Norwegian schools", *OECD Economics Department Working Paper* No. 661.

Calmfors, L. (2010), "Lessons from Sweden", paper presented at the Conference on Independent Fiscal Institutions, Budapest, 18-19 March.

Dahl, G.A., T. Birkeland Kloster, U. Larsen, K.J. Rakkestad, R. Reisvaag, B. Dyre Syverstern and C. Bolstad Træe (2011), "A cobweb model of financial stability in Norway", *Norges Bank Staff Memo* No. 15.

Hagemann, R. (2010), "Improving fiscal performance through fiscal councils", *OECD Economics Department Working Paper* No. 829.

Joumard, I., P. Hoeller, M. Pisu and D. Bloch (2012), "Less Income Inequality and more growth – Are they compatible; Part 3. Income redistribution via taxes and transfers across OECD countries", *OECD Economics Department Working Paper* No. 926.

Lorentzen, T. and E. Dahl (2006), "Active labour market programmes in Norway: are they helpful for social assistance recipients?", *Journal of European Social Policy*, Vol. 15, No. 1.

OECD (2008), *OECD Economic Survey of Norway, 2008*, OECD Publishing, Paris.

OECD (2010a), *OECD Economic Survey of Norway, 2010*, OECD Publishing, Paris.

OECD (2010b), "Sickness, Disability and Work: Breaking the Barriers", OECD Publishing, Paris.

OECD (2011), *G20 High-Level Principles on Financial Consumer Protection*, OECD, Paris. *www.oecd.org/dataoecd/58/26/48892010.pdf*.

Rønsen, M. and T. Skarohamar (2009), "Do welfare-to-work initiatives work? Evidence from an activation programme targeted at social assistance recipients in Norway", *Journal of European Social Policy*, Vol. 19, No. 1.

ANNEX A1

Taking stock of structural reforms

This table reviews recent action taken on recommendations from previous *Surveys*. Recommendations that are new in this *Survey* are listed in the relevant chapter.

Recommendations	Action taken since the previous *Survey* (March 2010)
A. Social protection	
Minimise work disincentives in the unemployment insurance system.	As an anti-crisis measure, the access to unemployment benefits for temporary laid-off workers was widened in 2009. The government proposes that this extension will be reversed from 2012 for new inflows.
	A special regulation, that enabled unemployed persons from age 62 to receive unemployment benefits until age 67, was abolished from 2011, with certain temporary transitional arrangements.
Reduce sick leave.	In July 2011, measures to provide for earlier and closer monitoring of sick leave were introduced, with provision for sanctions against the employee, employer and doctor for failure to follow up.
Tighten disability schemes.	The reform of the disability scheme announced in mid-2011 concentrated on technical adjustments to bring its provisions in line with those of old-age pensions but did not address the incentive and public spending problems.
B. Labour markets	
Increase flexibility in wage setting.	Backward action: The use of a mandatory extension of wage contracts with the objective of combating social dumping is introduced in the maritime construction industry, on construction sites, in the agriculture and garden centre industry and in the cleaning industry.
	Since 2010, there is joint and several liability related to minimum wages in sectors with mandatory extended wage contracts.
Modernise employment protection legislation.	No action.
Enhance efficiency of job placement services and ALMP.	The July 2006 merger of the Public Employment Services and the National Insurance Services was completed in early 2011; no efficiency gains have been visible as yet. The reform will be under evaluation until 2014.
C. Education	
Reduce the number of schools; improve accountability by publishing value-added assessment of school performance on standardised national tests of pupils.	No action to encourage reduction in school numbers, though some small schools are closing. Municipalities are required to make reports on their performance according to national indicators.
Introduce stricter selection and graduation criteria for initial teacher training; encourage formal training for developing competencies of practising teachers.	The required level of upper secondary school attainment for candidates for teacher training has been increased. A permanent system for the support of teachers' continuous professional development was established in 2009 and improved in 2011.
Develop more structured career paths with recognition for demonstrated competencies.	No action.

Recommendations	Action taken since the previous *Survey* (March 2010)
Include school performance as a determinant of school principals' rewards; consider school level merit-based salary awards to teachers.	No national action. Oslo education authorities have operated along these lines for several years.
Make the allocation of public funds to higher education institutions more transparent.	No action.
Introduce tuition fees and income-contingent repayment scheme in higher education.	No action.
D. Health care	
Reduce activity-based financing, and make greater use of co-payments by patients.	No action.
E. Financial markets	
Ensure competition in the banking sector.	After informal investigation the Competition Authority in February 2009 opened formal cases against Visa and Mastercard concerning debit and credit cards. The cases are pending before the Authority. To increase the competitiveness of savings banks compared with commercial banks, the government has proposed new regulations to allow savings banks to compete more effectively for equity and to allow easier structural changes – including mergers; regulations entered into force in July 2009.
Reduce vulnerabilities to the banking sector (*e.g.* introduce a limit on loan-to-value ratios, make the fees for the Deposit Guarantee Fund vary with banks' risk exposure).	In 2010, Finanstilsynet (Financial Supervisory Authority) introduced guidelines for prudent residential mortgage practice. Guidelines were further tightened in December 2011. The Ministry of Finance asked the Banking Law Commission to propose new legislation to facilitate more risk-sensitive fees to the Deposit Guarantee Fund.
F. Quality of public finance	
To raise the efficiency of public spending, evaluation tools such as regulatory impact analysis and cost-benefit analysis should be used more systematically.	No action. See also Chapter 1 of this *Survey*.
Tackle ageing issues.	The early retirement scheme in the public sector continues to strongly encourage workers to retire at age 62. A recent reform, effective in 2011, of the early retirement scheme in some parts of the private sector achieved actuarial neutrality at the margin, but at the cost of a significant public subsidy to these private sector workers.
Reform the tax system.	In 2009 and 2010, the valuation of housing in the base of the wealth tax was increased to 25% on owner-occupied property and 40% on rental property, which, given similar changes to the taxation of shares and business property, has at least not markedly reduced the preferential treatment of residential property. From 2011, the value-added tax base was extended to include electronic services delivered from abroad to private consumers in Norway. The 2012 budget will raise the value-added tax on food products by one percentage point, bringing it a step closer in line with the standard rate. See also Chapter 2 of this *Survey*.
Develop a multi-annual approach to budgetary planning.	No action. See also Chapter 1 of this *Survey*.
Create a fiscal council mandated to periodically evaluate budgetary developments.	In 2011, an Advisory Panel was set up to give "expert judgement and advice" on modelling and long-term simulation techniques, as well as on analyses reported to government and in budget reports. However, it lacks full independence and is not mandated to give judgement on the coherence between budgets and the "4% rule" guidelines.
G. Environmental policies	
Limit CO_2 emissions, and reduce the divergence of rates in the CO_2 tax.	The CO_2 tax has been extended to inland use of gas in 2010. The tax applies *inter alia* to heating and road transport. A road usage tax on biodiesel has been introduced. Incentives to buy cars with low CO_2 emissions have been strengthened. The CO_2 tax for mineral oil used in inland aviation will be adjusted for aviation covered by the EU ETS market.

Recommendations	Action taken since the previous *Survey* (March 2010)
Account systematically for environmental aspects in cost-benefit calculations (*e.g.* by using an explicit shadow price for GHG emissions).	The government has appointed an expert committee (expected to report by October 2012) with the task of evaluating and suggesting revisions of the current guidelines for cost-benefit analysis of public investments in Norway. Among the topics explicitly mentioned in the committee's mandate are environmental aspects in cost-benefit calculations including what shadow prices to associate with GHG emissions. See also Chapter 1 of this *Survey*.
H. Agriculture and fishery	
Enhance competition in the agriculture market.	No action.
Reduce tariffs and increase import quotas in the agriculture market.	Some new/increased import quotas have been put into effect from January 2012 due to the Article 19 agreement between Norway and the European Union from 2011.
Reduce restrictions on transfers of fishing quotas.	No action.
I. Support competition and reduce state aid	
Increase regulatory power of competition authorities.	No legislative action. An expert committee has been appointed to review experiences with the Competition Act and recommend necessary changes.
Increase competition and reduce barriers to entry.	No action.
Reduce state aid, public subsidies and tax distortions.	Budgetary support for industry has increased slightly. There has been a significant increase in actual payments to the renewable and clean energy sector.
Reduce state ownership in corporate Norway.	In connection with an acquisition, state ownership in Norsk Hydro ASA, a global supplier of aluminium, was reduced from 43% to 34%, although the government has permission to increase it to 40%. The government has initiated a process for considering changes in the ownership structure in Secora AS, a maritime contractor.
Improve state–owned activities governance.	A new White paper on the governance of state-owned enterprises passed through Parliament in June 2011.
Improve monitoring of cost–effectiveness of support for innovation and R&D.	As of 2011, the Ministry of Finance updated and revised the regulation of Skattefunn, the tax credit scheme for research and development. The revision implies a codification of practice as well as unification with the state aid regulations. An extensive comparison of the additionality and returns between the Norwegian R&D tax credit scheme and other innovation policy instruments was presented in 2008 as part of the evaluation of the R&D tax credit scheme. In an upcoming evaluation Technopolis Group and Statistics Norway will evaluate the Norwegian Research Council. The bulk of R&D grants to the business sector are extensively analysed annually.
J. Product market competition	
Promote competition in the postal services.	No action.
Reduce barriers to entry in the retail sector.	Backward actions: Exemptions to the Competition Act, allowing booksellers to set fixed prices for higher education books and literature have been extended (again) to the end of 2012 and 2014 respectively. Also an exemption allowing veterinaries to collectively bargain and enter into an agreement with the municipalities on both prices and level of service for veterinary services after normal working hours was prolonged to mid-2012. The Food Chain Committee has been looking at the relative strengths in the food value chain, resulting in the Official Norwegian Report: "Food, power and impotence." The follow-up of this report will be considered further in 2012.
Enhance efficiency in transport services.	The Competition Authority has introduced a new fare calculation system, the so-called parallel fare system, for all taxis in the country. The purpose is to make it easier for taxi customers to compare prices.

Chapter 1

Value for money and public spending

> *Norway attaches importance to efficiency and value for money in public spending, especially because of its high overall level. Reasonable guidelines for pursuing efficiency are in place and in some areas, for example tax collection, measures of efficiency show good performance. Information systems are increasingly in place that allow benchmarking of performance, especially across local government, but increased attention to outcome indicators is required as well. But the guidelines are not always followed in practice and the traditional Norwegian reliance on good sense and trust needs to be reinforced with strengthened arrangements for formal evaluation of projects and policies. Lengthening the time horizon for overall budgetary planning could help to improve the longer-term focus on value for money.*

Total public spending in Norway corresponds to just under half of GDP, around the average of the 32 members of the OECD. When expressed as a share of mainland GDP (excluding the output of the oil and gas sectors and international shipping) it rises to about 60%, the highest in the OECD (Figure 1.1). About half of this expenditure is transfers. The rest represents resources – wages and salaries, goods and services purchased and depreciation – provided directly by the public sector; such "production costs" amount to just over 30% of mainland GDP, the third highest behind Denmark and the Netherlands (Figure 1.2). Another way of looking at the importance of the public sector in Norway is by its direct share of employment which, when public corporations are included, is again the highest in the OECD (Figure 1.3).

The burden of financing public expenditure is moderated, compared with that in other OECD countries, by the return on accumulated petroleum revenues, which covers the cost of around one tenth of total expenditure. But, if management of resources in the public sector is less efficient than in the private sector, the potential excess costs are significant, as are the distortions to the mainland economy if a pervasive public sector presence were

Figure 1.1. **General government expenditures[1] as a percentage of GDP**

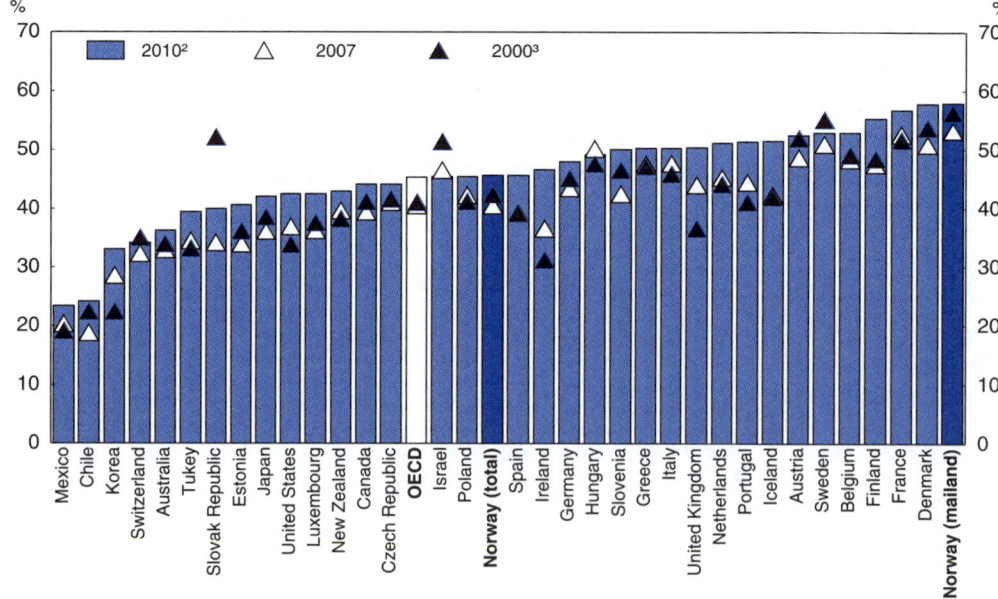

Note: OECD area is the simple average of countries for which data are available. The figure for Ireland excludes the one-off impact of recapitalisation in the banking sector (EUR 31.575 billion in 2010).
1. The data in this figure correspond to that in Figure 10 except that interest payments are included.
2. Or latest year available.
3. For Mexico: 2003 and for Turkey: 2006.
Source: OECD, National Accounts and OECD Economic Outlook Database.

StatLink ⟶ http://dx.doi.org/10.1787/888932572197

Figure 1.2. **Production costs of public spending as a percentage of GDP, 2010**[1]

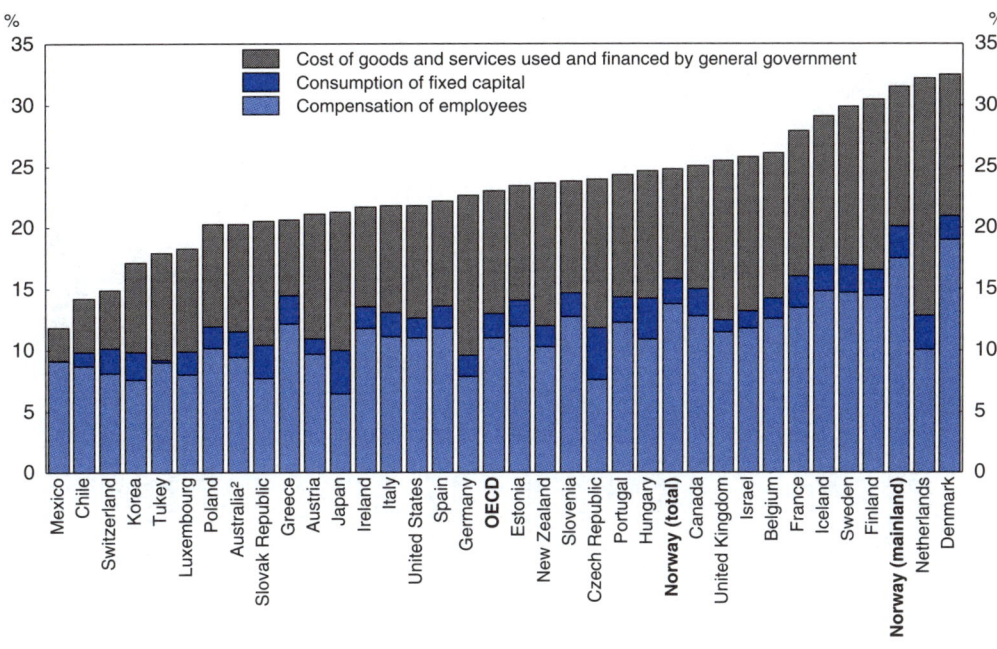

Note: OECD area is the simple average of countries for which data are available.
1. Or latest year available.
2. Data for Australia are based on a combination of Government Finance Statistics and National Accounts data provided by the Australian Bureau of Statistics.
Source: OECD National Accounts Database; Government at a Glance, 2011 and OECD Economic Outlook Database.

StatLink ⟶ http://dx.doi.org/10.1787/888932572216

to distort incentives. Equally, the potential benefits are high if expenditure is efficiently managed and fulfils a need that the private sector cannot.

Recent *Economic Surveys* have drawn attention to some areas of public spending where comparisons with other OECD countries suggest that spending could be more cost-effective. This is true of compulsory education (OECD, 2008) and also with some aspects of health care (OECD, 2010), with elements of environmental policies (OECD, 2010) and with the sickness and disability benefit schemes (OECD, 2005; 2010). Previous *Surveys* have suggested some specific ways in which policies in those areas could be made more cost-efficient.

In the case of school education, a key indicator of relative cost-efficiency is the performance of school children in internationally standardised tests, measured using the PISA study and compared with the amount of resources devoted to education. On this basis, while Norway's PISA scores are around the OECD average, expenditure on school education per student is perhaps 40% above average. More indirect measures of school performance, such as growth in the share of graduates in the population and the share of high-technology or engineering graduates in the total also show Norway lagging somewhat.

A number of possible explanations for these differences between Norway and other countries emerge. Teacher quality is one; the proportion of specialised teachers trained in mathematics and science is low, so that there is a risk that some children will be taught these subjects by teachers without a tertiary qualification. Another contributory factor is

1. VALUE FOR MONEY AND PUBLIC SPENDING

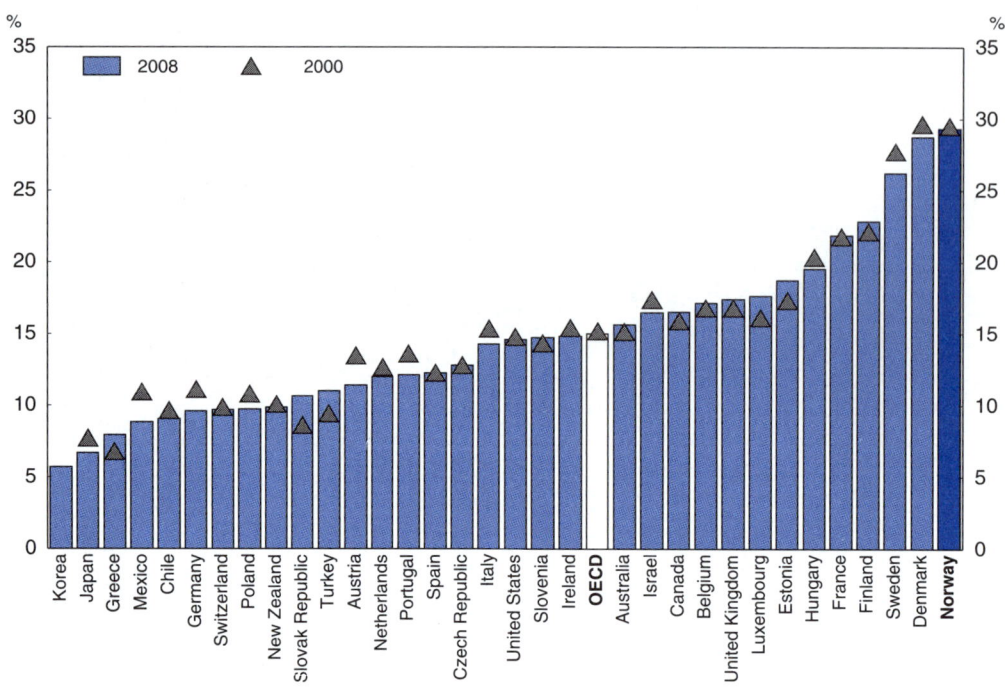

Figure 1.3. **Employment in general government and public corporations as percentage of the labour force**

Note: OECD area is the simple average of countries for which data are available. ILO data used in this figure is not comparable with national accounts data, hence cross-country comparisons may not be fully reliable.
Source: ILO and OECD, Government at a Glance, 2011.

StatLink ⟶ http://dx.doi.org/10.1787/888932572235

the relatively low pay of teachers, though total spending on teachers is high because of the high overall teacher-student ratio. Another finding worth recalling is the influence of average school size which is low in Norway. Both cross-country studies and Norway-specific research suggest that there are economies of scale in running schools.

In health spending, as in education, it is difficult to choose statistics which are a good representation of the overall performance of the system. A number of different cross-country indicators (such as life expectancy or amenable mortality compared with health care spending and lifestyle indicators) suggest that Norway could improve spending efficiency. Norway's position on this kind of ranking is not particularly poor, however. It is similar to that of Sweden and much better than that of Denmark or the United Kingdom, for example (see Joumard et al., 2010, Figure 6). It is also one of the best placed countries in the group with comparable system characteristics (Hungary, Ireland, Italy, New Zealand, Norway, Poland, United Kingdom). Nevertheless, The 2010 Economic Survey of Norway suggested, for example, that budgetary control in hospitals should be tightened and that activity based financing, in principle a good way of ensuring that resources are used where they are most useful, needed to be adjusted to prevent over-supply of some services.

Recent Surveys have also consistently picked out the sickness and disability benefit schemes as likely to be a source of excessive public spending, as discussed also in the Assessment and Recommendations chapter of this Survey. In many cases relevant recommendations concern changing policy to improve the incentives faced by individuals or companies, for example aligning carbon dioxide taxes to get a more cost-effective approach to greenhouse gas mitigation. They also often cover public sector accountability and the incentives faced by public sector actors themselves, such as recommending paying increased attention to performance indicators in education. The present chapter takes this last kind of issue further. It looks at the range of public spending in Norway from the point of view of what information, incentives and control mechanisms are present to ensure that managers of public spending themselves seek cost-efficient ways of reaching policy objectives.

Overall budgeting and expenditure planning

The 2002 *Economic Survey* of Norway, which also surveyed public expenditure (see also Joumard and Suyker, 2002) made three recommendations concerning the planning of overall public expenditure: to adopt a spending rule to reinforce the fiscal strategy, to move towards a management approach based on outcomes and to shift towards multi-annual budgeting. Instead of a spending rule, the "4% rule", which governs the mainland budget deficit (adjusted for the economic cycle), has been supplemented by the policy of maintaining an unchanged average level of taxation; over time, this has a broadly similar effect to a rule linking spending to growth in mainland national income – mainland GDP plus the real income from the Government Pension Fund Global (GPFG). Finally, the government has adopted the model of allocating expenditure based on outcomes to which it is directed, so that outcomes can be compared with plans, though in some areas of expenditure outcome indicators have yet to be fully defined.

Multi-annual budgeting could improve expenditure planning

The suggested move towards multi-annual budgeting was the subject of an official committee report during 2002, but was not adopted. Hence, the budgeting process has remained on an annual basis, but is nevertheless circumscribed. First by the 4% rule, which, though not embedded in the constitution, enjoys a wide degree of cross-party consensus (though not unanimity), and secondly by the current government's policy of requiring all changes in taxation to be revenue-neutral. This puts significant constraints on the range in which public expenditure can grow each year, even without formal multi-annual budgeting. The potential advantages of multi-annual budgeting are therefore not so much in terms of fiscal restraint, which is often the key consideration in other countries, as in better planning.

Annual budgeting means that, each year, spending authority in many areas lapses unless parliament passes a new budget. Each year, therefore, the Ministry of Finance has to negotiate with spending ministries to keep spending growth below limits determined by the 4% rule and the policy of keeping average tax levels unchanged. In order to try to direct spending towards the areas where it is most effective, each year ministries have to submit proposals for spending cuts, with the cuts to be redistributed to more favoured areas. In practice the process becomes a game between spending ministries and the finance ministry, as ministries propose cuts that they expect to be unacceptable to the government as a whole which are then rejected. Little redistribution of this sort typically takes place. This kind of process could be given more force if some annual cuts in ministerial allocations were made automatic instead of relying on ministries to suggest them. In Australia an "efficiency dividend" system works in this way. Ministries and agencies face a cut every year equal to a certain percentage (1¼ per cent, recently increased to 1½ per cent) of their operating costs. The resulting pool is available for redistribution across ministries.

The idea of multi-year budgeting is simply to get parliamentary approval, in some form, for spending for the out-years (i.e. more than one year ahead). This concerns not just total spending, for which the current policy of unchanged taxation combined with the 4% rule already provides quite good guidelines, but also spending on specific programmes. With some assurance that spending priorities will have some stability, this allows longer-term projects or programmes to be planned with some confidence in their continuity.

Other countries vary according to the degree of fixity of such programmes, but a number have moved towards quite binding allocations. For a large subset of expenditure, mainly excluding entitlement spending, the United Kingdom fixes spending allocations in nominal terms for five years; France uses a three-year horizon with the third year being indicative (this approach was used by the UK for some years before it recently switched to five years); in the Netherlands a fixed four-year cycle is used while Sweden employs a rolling three-year cycle, but with only the total spending being binding. A recent discussion document from the Irish Ministry of Finance proposes to have an annual budgeting process but to fix "Ministerial Expenditure Ceilings" in line with the aggregate spending limits derived from the (three-year) Stability Programme (Irish Ministry of Finance, 2011). Italy recently introduced rolling three-year budgets but the operation of the new system has been overshadowed by the financial crisis which has necessitated significant annual revisions leading to successively tighter spending plans.

In some cases there would be little difference in practice. Firstly, entitlement-driven spending, such as social security or health care, is not controlled directly. The factors that determine it are not likely to vary much from one year to the next. Over the long term bigger changes can occur, notably through the ageing of the population. Specifically budgeting for such long-term changes would be impossible, but the Ministry of Finance does long-term spending projections in order to consider what policy changes may be needed in future to deal with such challenges.

Secondly, the current process of annual budgeting as outlined above leads in practice to rather rigid ministerial budgets in relative terms. Planners may have to take account of the possibility that spending limits may change from one year to the next, but in practice this rarely happens; spending planners need predictability in resource allocations rather than rigidity. Ministries have some inter-year flexibility, in that up to 5% of operating expenses can be carried over from one year into the next.

Most countries do some form of multi-annual indicative budgeting, but this is usually limited (as in Norway's case) to projections of spending and revenue under unchanged policies, usually at a rather aggregate level, rather than a strong commitment to implement specific spending plans; decisions in the annual budgets are not constrained by the projections from the previous exercise.

The main gains for Norway from multi-annual budgeting are therefore likely to be: i) inducing politicians to take a slightly longer view of policy planning; ii) allow ministries to switch some effort towards planning effective policy strategies instead of the annual struggle for resources with other spending ministries and the Ministry of Finance; and iii) allowing spending on some projects to vary more from year to year without the risk of funds being lost if they are not spent. The extent of these gains would vary according to how long a budgeting period was actually selected. The costs would be mainly the reduced flexibility to respond to unexpected events, though, as in the current system, a contingency reserve should be able to cover many such developments. There may also be some costs due the additional effort required to get inter-ministerial agreement for a longer period.

An initial step could be to switch from the current system of presenting out-year projections of expenditure under unchanged policies, to presenting expenditure allocations for three years. The presumption would be that the first year is definitive, as under the current system, that the second year is fixed unless extraordinary circumstances arise, and that the annual budget would focus mainly on rolling the programme forward one year. Expenditure would be allocated at the level of each ministry, and could also be specified at a more detailed level. Such a system would give some gains under item i) above but might not achieve much under item ii). Another possibility would be to move to a much more fixed approach in which the budgetary period was longer than one year, allowing ministries to switch funds between years, and perhaps across programmes, within their fixed overall level of funding, as they wished. In theory this might give much greater gains, but would also probably be too large an organisational step to contemplate at the moment.

Any change in budget procedures must conserve the essential elements of the current approach to macroeconomic policy, which is the 4% rule. Applying this over a longer period would be more difficult than currently, where the 4% is applied to the value of the Government Pension Fund Global (GPFG) at the end of the previous year. The principal guideline, that the mainland structural budget deficit is to be equal to 4% of the value of the GPFG over time, but not in any particular year, would be unaffected. But some smoothing of the increased spending permitted by the growing value of the GPFG would be helpful. In addition, a more explicit understanding that significant deviations from the rule, either over- or under-spending, should (macroeconomic conditions permitting) be followed in subsequent budgets with a period of the opposite bias, would help to keep the value of the GPFG on track.

There may be some undesirable side effects

Multi-year budgeting has some potential problems. One key danger is that it could bias public spending upwards. This could happen if, in any one year, the planned spending level for that year were treated as a floor in the case of a shortfall of resources for some external reason, but were not treated as a ceiling when circumstances were more favourable than expected.

Although this may be a danger, and is one of the reasons that multi-year budgeting was not adopted after being considered in 2002, it is not inevitable. The idea of multi-year budgeting is that spending plans should be legislated in a medium-term context. If that context requires that spending should not grow too fast, either for reasons of macroeconomic balance or for fiscal prudence, this would form part of the debate in the parliament. Such a debate could anchor prudence more reliably than the current annual debate about the appropriate fiscal stance. It is therefore time to reconsider the issue, especially in the light of the number of countries that have moved in this direction since 2002.

Other aspects of the current system would need only little modification. With spending plans fixed, unanticipated variations in revenue or spending needs, to the extent that they exhausted the contingency reserve, would have to be accommodated through variations in use of the GPFG (or in taxation). This is already the case at the moment, as the 4% rule sets the expected structural deficit, allowing automatic stabilisers to work fully within the budget year. With a longer-time horizon, the policy on average tax levels could remain unchanged, though there are arguments that economic efficiency could improve if their level could be reduced over time. Either of these approaches could be incorporated into a multi-annual plan, and automatic stabilisers would work as they do now.

There appears to be no strong demand for longer-term planning from spending ministries, though in individual cases civil servants would prefer, other things being equal, a long planning horizon. Apart from the possibility that longer-term planning is a bad idea, there are a number of likely explanations for this. Firstly, individual ministries may feel that annual negotiations give them more opportunities for lobbying for extra resources, even though this cannot work for all ministries taken together. Secondly, ministries are obviously well adapted to the current system and, in a context of generally growing public expenditure, quite large changes from year to year in the relative priority given to different projects or policies can occur without significant actual spending cuts anywhere. Thirdly, having been rejected in 2002, it may seem unachievable.

Finally, local governments[1] may find that annual budgeting at the central government level is a constraint on their planning. Local governments are required to balance their budgets year-by-year, except for borrowing to finance investment.

Aiming at value for money

As outlined earlier, previous *Economic Surveys* have suggested some policy areas where Norway's visible results appear to fall short of what could be expected given the amount being spent. Education policy is one, some aspects of health spending may be another; the sickness and disability schemes are discussed in the Assessment and Recommendations of this *Survey*. Norway has a number of characteristics that have to be borne in mind when assessing efficiency in public spending. It has a relatively small population of 5 million, distributed unevenly in a large area (World Bank data show that among OECD countries only Canada, Australia and Iceland have a lower average population density; New Zealand's population density is very close but slightly higher). Mountains or fjords or both separate many of the population centres. Norway's national identity is historically particularly linked to the coastal areas in the south-west, west and north, quite remote from the capital.

Aside from these geographical features, Norwegians appear to favour redistribution, despite having a distribution of income (pre-taxes and benefits) that displays less inequality than most other OECD countries (see Figure 1). This concern for equity carries through attitudes to the provision of public services, especially of health and education, where the idea that everyone should have equal access to these services, regardless of where they live, is quite widely shared.

It is also the case that quite a lot of public sector policy is developed or managed in a decentralised way, through local government, though in some cases, concerns over cost-effectiveness have brought some recentralisation recently. This recentralisation has occurred in the case of hospitals, which used to be run at county level but returned to central management in 2006, and some labour market and social benefits following the progressive integration of national social insurance offices with local labour market services since 2008 (the "NAV" reform).

A need for greater transparency? The case of regional policy

These features mean that cross-country comparisons may show that spending in certain policy areas seems high by international standards because of regional policy, not because of spending inefficiency. It is therefore important to have a clear idea of what the objectives and costs of regional policy are. It has been very difficult to estimate the costs of regional policy, for example an OECD survey of regional policy (OECD, 2007) was able to list a number of measures directed to regional policy but not to provide an overall cost estimate. The annual budget documentation includes an annex detailing a large number of items directed to regional policy objectives but legislated under many other headings. Table 1.1 (identical to Table 3, repeated here for convenience) summarises some information from that document and some estimates of additional costs.

Agriculture is more heavily subsidised in Norway than in almost any other OECD country. Direct non-production-related subsidies are included in the budget documentation. In addition, implicit subsidies through market price support – calculated by the OECD as the Producer Subsidy Estimate – totalled about 22 billion NOK, about 1.1% of mainland GDP, in 2010; the entry in Table 1.1 is an arbitrary half of this. Education absorbs the equivalent of about 8% of mainland GDP and it has been estimated (Bonnesrønning et al., 2008) that increasing the average school size from 200 to 400 pupils would reduce costs by 5 to 6%, or approximately 0.5% of mainland GDP; regional policy is not the only reason for small average school size so an arbitrary one fifth of this amount is included in the table. Other items for which even rudimentary cost estimates are not available but which would be likely to be significant are health service costs and transport infrastructure investment costs (Table 1.1 includes current subsidies, but capital investment subsidies have not been estimated).

Hence, regional policy absorbs resources equivalent to at least 2½ per cent of mainland GDP, or more than a third of total expenditure on education. Only three quarters of this appears as spending in the budget. More than a third of the total, and more than one half of the identified "off-budget" estimates, is provided through subsidies to agriculture. This is at least as much as, and maybe much more than, the budgeted total for the main explicit regional policy instrument – the implicit wage subsidy through reduced contributions and taxes.

Though this information can be extracted from budgetary documentation, its presentation could be given greater transparency. Much of this expenditure may be accurately targeted, but if the objective of regional policy is essentially to encourage employment in certain areas, the amount delivered through agricultural policy is not likely to be well-targeted. Some will certainly increase employment but much will go into increasing rents or land prices and a higher capital intensity of production.

Transparency can potentially improve efficiency, simply by drawing attention to policy areas that are absorbing a lot of resources. For instance, Table 1.1 suggests the question as to whether the aims of regional policy would be better served by reducing support to agriculture and switching those resources to increasing the subsidy to wages in remote regions.[2] Bringing information on spending together in this way should also help to identify more precisely what the aims of regional policy are and how it can be established whether they are being met. In a similar way, it would be useful to collate expenditure, including implicit expenditure, on environmental policy across different ministries to be

Table 1.1. **Budgeting for regional policy**

Item	2011 budget allocation or estimated implicit cost	
	NOK billion	% mainland GDP
Budget figure for the cost of regional policy	34.4	1.7
of which:		
Reduced social contributions		
Private sector	7.0	0.4
Public sector	5.2	0.3
Reduced income tax and other measures for Finnmark and North Troms	1.2	0.1
Reduced tax on energy, district and other grants in northern Norway	3.9	0.2
Direct subsidies to agriculture	11.5	0.6
Transport and other infrastructure subsidies	2.6	0.1
Public services, environment	2.2	0.1
Capital costs of road and other infrastructure investment	??	??
Other implicit costs:		
Subsidies to agriculture via Producer Subsidy Estimate	4.5	0.3
Education	2.0	0.1
Total	40.9	2.1

Sources: Ministry of Finance (2010); 1) Introductory section; 2) Table 1.2; 3) Table 1.1; 4) Table 1.3; 5) Table 1.4; 6) Table 1.5; 7) Table 1.6. Other items are OECD estimates, see text.

able to assess costs and outcomes against the governments overall sustainable development objectives (OECD, 2010).

The fact that a policy absorbs resources or even that cost information is not easily available does not in itself mean that the money is inefficiently spent. More than transparency is needed for keeping costs down, however; mechanisms for aiming directly at efficiency are needed.

One can divide mechanisms to promote spending efficiency into two broad, and to some extent overlapping, classes: those that set incentives so that the best options should be chosen by decentralised decision makers; and those that analyse costs (and benefits) *ex ante* and select the best option.

Incentives for efficiency

Little use of performance-based rewards for civil servants

Use of direct incentives for efficiency is patchy. The move towards output-based budgeting described earlier could in principle allow public sector workers' pay to be linked to their performance in a wide range of contexts. For some time, some use of this idea has been made at the higher levels of management. Most ministries are structured such that policy implementation is delegated to agencies whose head may be employed on a contract with performance-related rewards. Only a small minority of civil servants are employed directly in ministries rather than in agencies.

The agencies themselves operate under annual "contracts" (in the Letter of Allocation from ministries to agencies) which specify performance objectives. According to Loegreid *et al.* (2005), in a survey of practice in 2005, the performance objectives at that time would be difficult to use in a reward/punishment scheme because they were often too numerous or too qualitative or imprecise. Loegreid *et al.* (2005) also reported that this form of management was not working very effectively because agencies that fell short of (or exceeded) objectives did not systematically see their resource allocation reduced (increased), although there was some tendency for this to occur. This observation does not really provide the right information for assessing whether the system is encouraging efficiency, since the incentives should be faced by individual managers not necessarily by the agency itself (unless there are different agencies competing to implement the same policy).

In response to the problem of the excessive length of Letters of Allocation, they were tending to become shorter but also more general "and more binding" after 2000 (Loegreid et al., 2005). A rather general specification of aims suits a system where decision-making is delegated with a considerable degree of trust that the agency will seek to meet those aims in a cost-efficient way. Performance reward systems could be used at a lower level where more precise definition of "outputs" is feasible. As in many countries, little use is made of this possibility at the moment with some exceptions at managerial levels. This is the result of a combination of unwillingness to compromise the civil servant work ethic with monetary incentives and the unsuitability of available "output" information. The Budget Department in the Ministry of Finance monitors whether ministries spend money according to plans, and examines new policy initiatives, but has only a limited role in assessing value for money in ministries' implementation of agreed policies.

Sharing performance information

In the public sector, simply making good information on outcomes available can improve performance and good information is in any case a pre-requisite for assessing individual or collective performance. But in many ways there has been a reluctance to use explicit information on performance.

The case of school education in Norway is an example where setting up and making use of a system to provide information on student performance, and to use it to help improve teaching, has proved difficult (see OECD, 2008 and 2011a). National standardised tests provide information on students' ability at the beginning of a school year, useful information for planning teaching.

Part of the Ministry of Education's efforts to improve efficiency includes requiring municipalities to provide regular annual reports on school performance. In the first years of this programme, very few municipalities submitted such reports and the ministry has had to work to get them interested in developing and discussing the quality reports. Unlike most municipalities in Norway, the Oslo school system uses a set of school- and pupil-level indicators to assess performance of school principals and for school principals to assess performance of their teachers. School principals also have more managerial freedom than in many municipalities. This approach has been in place for some years (OECD, 2008), but as yet there is no statistical analysis to assess the Oslo municipality's claim that results and efficiency have improved with this system.

A more sensitive and different kind of example of where better information might improve performance, but where the current setting of incentives might result in the opposite effect, is in the sickness and disability benefit systems. Since general indicators of health and life expectancy in Norway are above average, the high levels of sickness and disability are as much a reflection of incentives in the benefit system as of need. It seems likely that there is some implicit collusion where the system is used by employers to dismiss low-productivity workers.

Efforts over the past decade to change the incentives of the actors involved (employer, employee, employee's doctor, social security office) have failed to reduce take-up of these benefits, to the detriment of the supply of labour and the budget. One reason for this may be that as yet no priority has been given to verification of doctors' diagnoses, either at the initial stage or at any follow up stage. A new system will give doctors access to a database of all doctors' decisions in various circumstances, allowing them to benchmark their own decisions. This database should also be used to identify doctors whose decisions may seem biased and bring in independent verification with potential sanctions. Otherwise it is quite likely that doctors who are currently stricter than average (but may not be aware of this) will feel pressured to certify sickness or disability more easily.

Local government: the KOSTRA system

There has been a lot of progress in information sharing among local governments. The KOSTRA system gives individual municipalities ready access to budgeting information from all other municipalities for the purposes of comparison. This information is quite detailed so that it can be seen not just how much money municipalities spend on different programmes but also how they spend it. Figure 1.4 shows how Bergen municipality can compare itself with other large cities on a variety of social welfare indicators, for example. This is very useful and few other countries have such a system; academics have access to the data and can conduct useful research into policy effectiveness. The ten largest municipalities also participate in a system called ASSS-Teamwork where members meet regularly, using KOSTRA and other data, to compare their performance.

For the future development of the system an important element to bear in mind is the difference between input and outcome indicators; some measures that are really detailed input indicators may seem as though they can be treated as outcomes. For example, the money spent on kindergartens is clearly an input variable and the number of places provided for children would be an output. From one point of view this is indeed the relevant output indicator, since national policy has mandated municipalities to provide kindergarten places for all children of a certain age. A measure of municipal efficiency would be the cost per kindergarten place provided, which KOSTRA can show.

However, the ultimate objective of this policy is to improve educational and labour market outcomes for children, and also facilitate labour market access for parents. From this perspective the number of kindergarten places is an intermediate input (or output) variable, but not an objective in itself. This issue applies in almost any policy area, for example progress in higher education is currently often measured by the share of graduates in the population. This is not a criticism of KOSTRA, which seems an excellent system. It is rather a reminder of some limits on what it can be expected to do.

Central government: StatRes

Corresponding to KOSTRA at the level of central government is an information system called StatRes. There would appear to be much less use of this type of data by ministries and agencies to try to benchmark themselves on practices elsewhere than there is of KOSTRA by local government. This is partly because, while all local governments tend to have the same functions, the input indicators that are relevant to ministries may all be similar but the outcome indicators should be very different in many cases. Some central government responsibilities can be looked at in this way, however. Edvardsen *et al.* (2010) use Data Envelopment Analysis to produce estimates of efficiency variation across higher

Figure 1.4. **Inter-municipality comparisons of social welfare indicators, 2009**

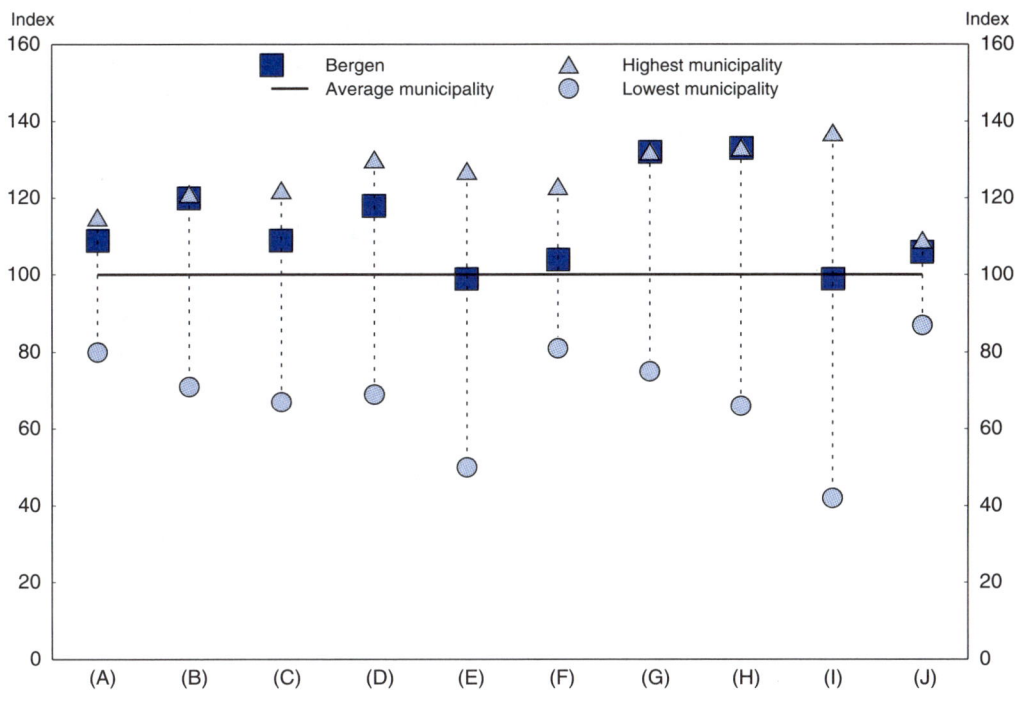

Note: (A): Use of resources.
(B): Net spending on social services per inhabitant aged 18-66.
(C): Net spending on benefits per inhabitant aged 18-66.
(D): Ratio of recipients to population aged 18-66.
(E): Ratio of recipients to population aged 18-24.
(F): Gross social benefit spending per recipient.
(G): Average period of dependency on social welfare.
(H): Share of recipients receiving benefit for over 6 months.
(I): Sick leave.
(J): Employee satisfaction index.
Source: Bergen Department of Finance, *Competition and Ownership*.

StatLink ⟶ http://dx.doi.org/10.1787/888932572254

education institutions and hospitals, as well as estimates of productivity growth. One way of using this information is to estimate potential efficiency savings if all institutions could be brought up to some standard. For example, in tertiary education it is estimated that potential efficiency gains could save between 13% and 33% of total person hours, or in police services between 15% and 26% (Edvardsen *et al.*, 2010).

A more practical use of StatRes data (since such DEA analysis does not identify what measures can be taken to achieve these savings) is that such analysis can show which institutions have relatively high or relatively low apparent efficiency, so that possible factors affecting efficiency can be identified. Background factors can affect apparent productivity but be outside the control of the institution. Used with care, nevertheless, such research can provide pointers; cross-country comparisons, for example, have identified the above-average numbers of doctors and nurses per head of population in Norway as a possible source of high costs (Erlandsen, 2008; OECD, 2010). Estimated changes on productivity levels in particular sectors might also help to identify impacts of policy changes.

StatRes is managed by the Statistical Office using information supplied by ministries, and data is published with some delay. Some of the limitations of StatRes data appear to be related to the lack of incentive for ministries and agencies to provide the data – which is available in ministries themselves much earlier – in a timely fashion and at a suitable level of disaggregation. As Edvardsen *et al.* (2010) point out, it may be difficult to provide appropriate incentives for data production, especially when it is left up to each ministry to decide on its own policy.

High levels of efficiency are achieved in some areas – tax collection

One agency where results have been very good in cross-country comparison is in tax collection. As a share of revenue collected, costs in Norway are below those of most OECD countries and have been falling (Figure 1.5). High levels of taxation from oil, where the number of individual taxpayers is low, as well as a general culture of tax compliance, may partly explain this, but a relatively simple tax system and cost-effective collection methods must also be contributory factors.

Figure 1.5. **Ratio of aggregate tax administration costs per 100 units of net revenue collection**

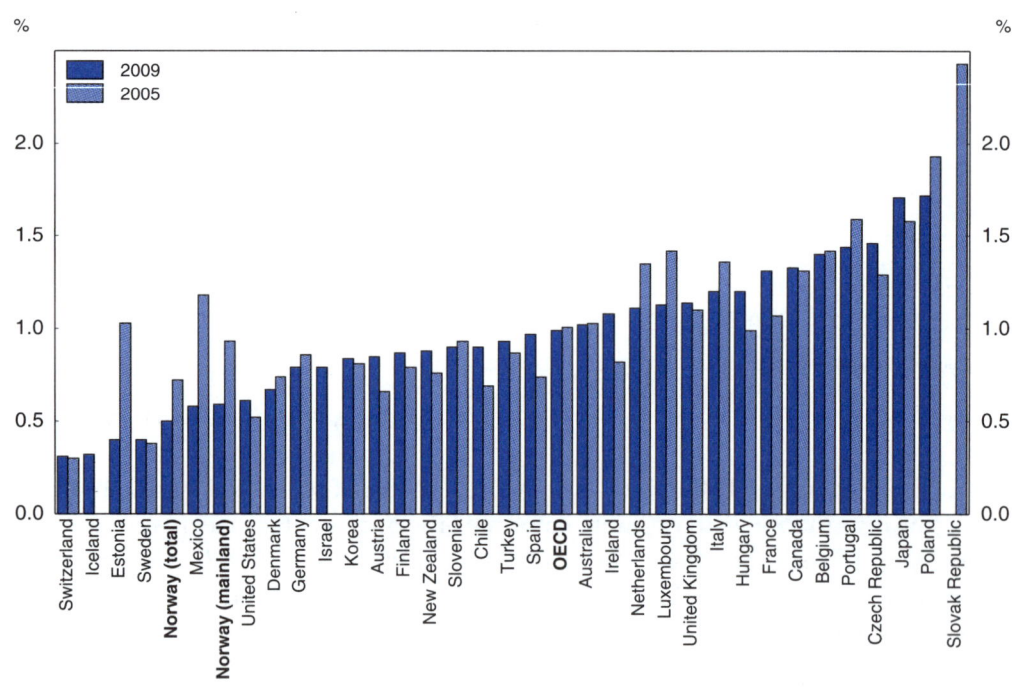

Note: Data for Norway (mainland) refer to mainland revenue only. This is an upper limit, calculated by assuming that administrative costs on non-mainland revenue were zero. The OECD area is the simple average of countries for which data are available.
Source: OECD, *Government at a Glance*, 2011 and Secretariat calculations.

StatLink http://dx.doi.org/10.1787/888932572273

Incentives for efficiency: using the private sector as a benchmark

The system of management of public expenditure in Norway does allow extensive use of one method of benchmarking for efficiency – use of the private sector. Public procurement spending is delegated quite widely with departmental managers generally being responsible for their own budgets and therefore having strong incentives to minimise costs. By international comparison, Norway is around average in its overall use of outsourcing (Figure 1.6), though well behind countries such as the Netherlands and the United Kingdom.

The pattern of outsourcing varies widely across countries. In Norway a relatively small proportion of total expenditure outsourced is on that financed by general government but provided by the private sector, though for a number of countries this is even smaller. This may reflect the general preference in Norway for public services to be provided by publicly-owned bodies rather than sub-contracted to private-sector companies. This is despite the fact that the benefits of taking advantage of the private sector's greater experience with keeping costs down are not just theoretical – there is some direct evidence from Norwegian experience.

The Norwegian Institute of Transport Economics has looked at a small number of road construction projects fully outsourced to the private sector, through public-private-partnership (PPP) schemes. Overall monetary costs did not seem to be reduced by the involvement of the private sector, but construction times were significantly reduced (Eriksen et al., 2007). The reduction in construction time may not have given any direct

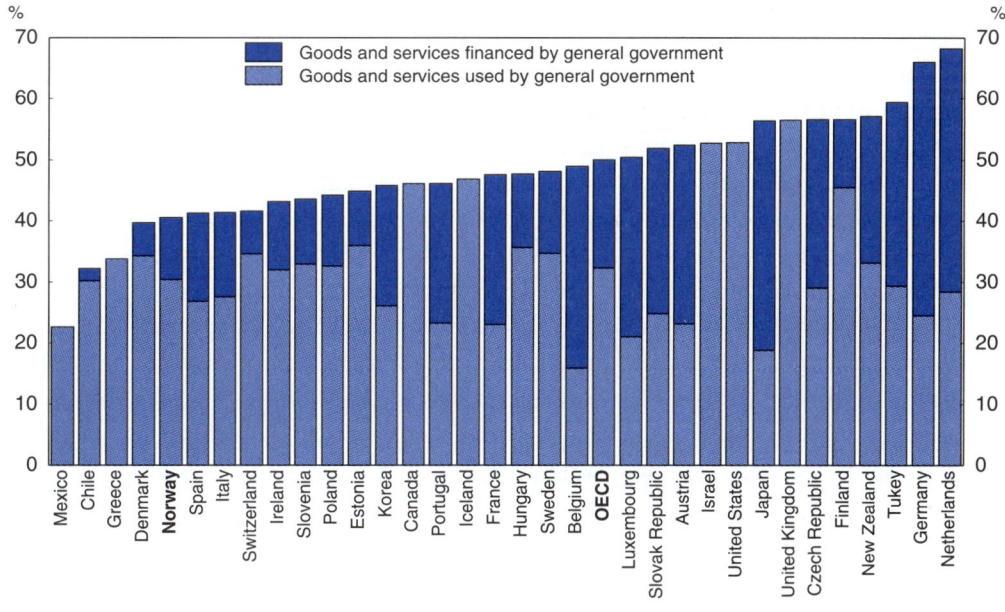

Figure 1.6. **Expenditure on general government outsourcing**
As a percentage of final government consumption expenditure, 2010[1]

Note: OECD area is the simple average of countries for which data are available. The goods and services used by general government are the intermediate consumption component of government outsourcing and include the procurement of intermediate products required for government production such as accounting of information technology (IT) services. The goods and services financed by government reflect social transfers in kind via market producers (including those that are initially paid for by citizens but are ultimately refunded by government, such as medical treatments refunded by public social security payments).
1. Or latest year available.
Source: OECD National Accounts Database.

StatLink ⇒ http://dx.doi.org/10.1787/888932572292

budgetary savings for the government, but it is likely to have reduced the broader costs of the projects (through reduced disruption to traffic flows) and is therefore a clear benefit.

PPPs themselves have become somewhat controversial, as part of their attraction in other countries has been the opportunity they give – when private financing is part of the contract – for provision of extra public services with little immediate budgetary impact. But pure financing gains are essentially illusory and, more likely, financing costs are actually higher since borrowing costs for the private sector are typically higher than for the public sector. Strong evidence for this comes from the United Kingdom where off-budget liabilities amounting to some 2½ per cent of GDP have built up under the Private Finance Initiative (House of Commons, 2011). The excess cost of private finance has increased a lot since the financial crisis, but was present even before it. The financing side of all projects should remain fully accounted for in public budgets.

UK experience shows that cost reductions can come from private sector involvement, especially in reduced construction costs but also through greater certainty of costs when construction cost risk is transferred to the private sector. However, care should be taken in transferring other kinds of risk to the private sector since this is likely to be priced in to the contracts and, unless the risk is genuinely better managed by the private sector than the public sector, could increase overall costs. UK experience suggests that other forms of partnership, such as turnkey construction or maintenance contracts, are sufficient to provide the key incentives for cost-reduction (House of Commons, 2011).

Experience from provision of kindergartens in Norway also suggests that private sector involvement can lower the cost of providing services, without compromising quality. A Ministry of Education study shows that cost per hour of care appears to be 10% lower in privately-run kindergartens than in municipal ones (Ministry of Education, 2009, Table 12). Ensuring that quality of care is comparable is one difficulty in making such comparisons. One municipality reported that one use it made of KOSTRA was to realise that it had been using more highly qualified staff in its kindergartens than elsewhere and it made savings by lowering the required level of qualifications. Overall, however, it seems likely that private care is at least as good as that from the public sector – a survey of parents showed that satisfaction levels were higher with private sector than public sector provision (EPSI, 2010). This was more due to value for money than the quality of care; quality of care was rated somewhat higher for private provision than for public provision but the gap was much less than that for value for money, corroborating the Ministry of Education study.

Kindergarten provision by municipalities has risen rapidly in recent years, following research in Norway and elsewhere showing that it can improve educational outcomes later in life. The expansion has been driven by national policy mandated to municipalities. Around half of the kindergarten places in Norway are now provided by the private sector. This is unusual in public services, especially in education, where the role of the private sector is very low. The reason for this exception in kindergarten provision is partly because municipalities found it difficult to expand public provision sufficiently rapidly, but also because the ministerial directive made it clear that municipalities should consider private provision on equal terms with the public sector. This is a good example of using research results on costs and benefits to influence policy, and contrasts with the lack of assessment applied to Oslo's performance-based reward system in school education, mentioned earlier.

In health care, too, there is very little use of private provision. Use of DRG-based (Diagnostic Related Groups) financing in decentralised management of hospitals had mixed results and, partly as a result of this, hospital management has been brought back into the control of central government (OECD, 2010). Other countries, such as France, which also have a strong tradition of delivering public services through public providers, do manage to combine this with significant private provision in both school education and health care.

Expenditure assessment tools

The management of policy assessment

Norway's public administration makes use of the normal set of tools for optimising public expenditure. Current guidelines for Regulatory Impact Assessment (RIA) and Cost Benefit Analysis (CBA) were introduced or revised around the turn of the century and are based on OECD recommended practice. International comparisons of Norway's situation in this area are mixed, however. For example, according to OECD's *Government at a Glance* (indicator No. 47) Norway is one of only six OECD countries where an *ex post* assessment of RIA is mandatory, yet civil servants and academics in Norway tend to argue that RIA use leaves much to be desired, despite the establishment of a panel to support its use. RIA is concerned with the wider impact of government policy, not just direct public spending, but it can have an important impact on spending efficiency nevertheless.

One difficulty is likely to be that it is no-one's clear responsibility to ensure that RIA guidelines are followed, or to monitor the quality of the assessments that are carried out. Many countries have given responsibility for this to a specific ministry or agency, which has potential authority, or at least oversight, over practices in all ministries. For example, it may need to be consulted when new policies are being developed, conduct its own RIA, or issue reports on individual ministries. The number of countries where the regulatory oversight authority has these kind of function has been steadily increasing and includes most of Norway's neighbours (Figure 1.7; Table 1.2).

As Table 1.2 shows, Norway does have a ministry responsible for overall progress on regulatory reform but this ministry, currently the Ministry for Government Administration, Reform and Church Affairs, has none of the prerogatives to look into practice and outcomes in other ministries that are given to its counterparts in many other countries. The ministry oversees the Agency for Public Management and eGovernment (Difi), established in 2008, which aims to strengthen the government's work in renewing the Norwegian public sector and improve the organisation and efficiency of government administration. The agency concentrates on facilitating productivity improvements throughout the public sector, for example in promoting co-ordinated use of ICT, or setting up public procurement procedures.

Difi has experts on cost-benefit analysis and policy assessment but it seems they may be under-used. The Ministry of Government Administration issued the guidelines for RIA and CBA referred to earlier and, following dissatisfaction with the use of RIA, a panel to support ministries in using it was set up, first experimentally and then (in 2009) permanently (OECD, 2010). But the ministry itself still has no role in seeing that its own guidelines are being followed and while ministries are free to seek help from the RIA panel,

Figure 1.7. **Increasing use of a regulatory oversight body at the central government level (1998, 2005 and 2008)**

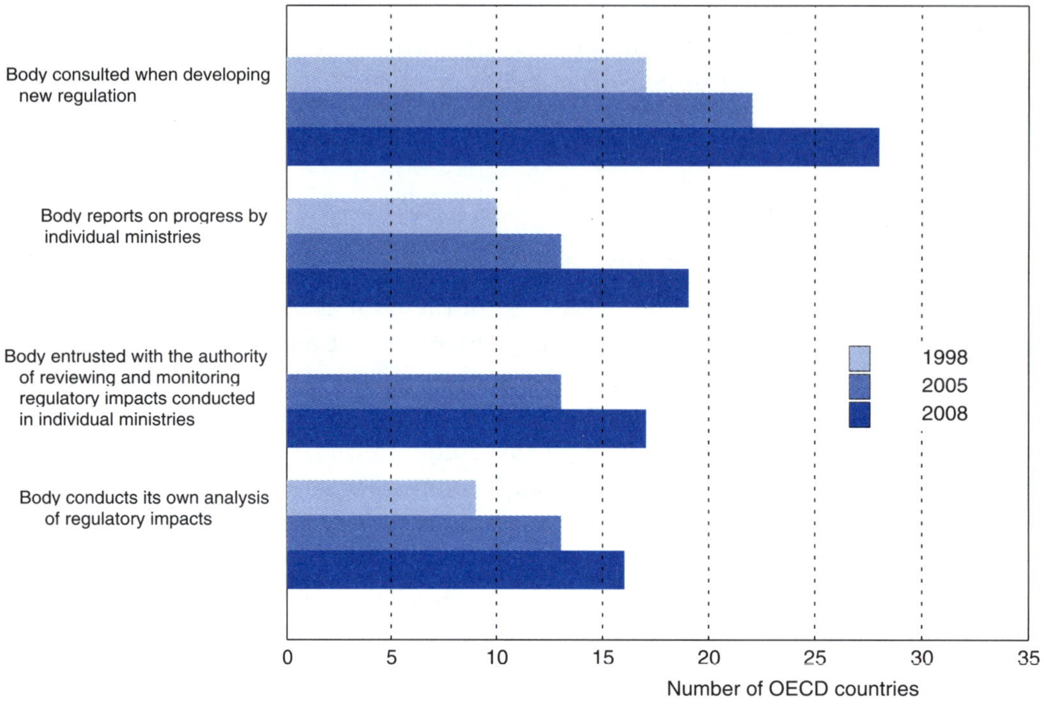

Source: OECD Government at a Glance, 2011.

StatLink ⟶ http://dx.doi.org/10.1787/888932572311

Table 1.2. **Aspects of government regulatory oversight authority (2008)**

Central government regulatory oversight authority:	Countries with this provision
• Is consulted as part of the process of developing new regulation	Australia, Austria, Belgium, Canada, Czech Republic, Denmark, Estonia, Finland, France, Germany, Hungary, Iceland, Ireland, Italy, Japan, Korea, Luxembourg, Mexico, Netherlands, New Zealand, Poland, Portugal, Slovak Republic, Slovenia, Sweden, Switzerland, United Kingdom, United States, Russian Federation. Norway – no.
• Reports on progress made on reform by individual ministries	Australia, Austria, Belgium, Canada, Denmark, Germany, Iceland, Italy, Japan, Korea, Mexico, Netherlands, Portugal, Slovak Republic, Spain, Sweden, Switzerland, United Kingdom, United States. Norway – no.
• Minister is accountable for promoting government-wide progress on regulatory reform	Australia, Austria, Belgium, Canada, Czech Republic, Denmark, Estonia, Finland, France, Germany, Greece, Hungary, Iceland, Ireland, Italy, Japan, Korea, Mexico, Netherlands, Norway, Poland, Portugal, Slovak Republic, Slovenia, Spain, Sweden, United Kingdom, United States, Russian Federation. Norway – yes.

Note: This table covers 3 of 11 relevant indicators in Government at a Glance. The average number of "yes" entries per country is just under 6; Norway has one "yes".
Source: OECD (2011), Table 45.3: http://dx.doi.org/10.1787/888932392267.

they are not obliged to do so. There does not seem to have been an improvement in use of RIA since the panel was established. One of the most important shortcomings is that the policy development process does not sufficiently respect the requirement to consider – early in the process – alternative ways of meeting the policy aims.

The use of cost-benefit analysis

Cost-benefit analysis is more directly concerned with public spending efficiency than RIA, but, with the important exception of the Quality Assurance Scheme discussed later, the situation concerning quality control of analysis carried out in line ministries is rather similar. There have been a number of reports into the use of CBA in recent years but there is still dissatisfaction and a wide-ranging inquiry is currently under way which is scheduled to report in late 2012. Apparent anomalies include that CBA applied to hospital provision has to take into account land costs but not travel costs for patients and workers and, where travel costs are a relevant factor, there is no standard shadow price used for greenhouse gas emissions, despite the importance of this as a policy target in Norway (OECD, 2010); instead, the price used depends on the policy goal. It is true that, in both of these cases, neglect of these factors is quite likely to reduce nominal government spending, but would not help policy targets to be efficiently pursued. The current guidelines allow line ministries to set their own prices for externalities, so that, for example, the price of a statistical life, a key parameter for anything involving health and safety, can vary across ministries.

In another example, according to the Ministry of Government Administration, CBA carried out in the Ministry of Transport on road construction projects shows that very few (perhaps none) of the projects that the ministry implements have benefits which exceed costs. This does not mean that all projects are carried out regardless of cost; most projects submitted for CBA are in fact rejected. But, along with frequent complaints about road quality and capacity in Norway, it does suggest that current CBA procedures may not be a very effective way of filtering projects. Project choices are not entirely random, however, some research has shown that relevant components of CBA are correlated with choice of project, even if net benefits themselves are not the clear criterion.

One problem with CBA in road projects is that the model used in the Ministry of Transport for assessing costs and benefits appears to analyse only the immediate costs and benefits of the project, including reduced journey times and taking some account of likely increased traffic generated. But it does not attempt to assess the impact on economic development of affected areas. Quite plausibly, these effects would be highly correlated with estimates of increased traffic, but they may be greater than the private benefit associated with extra journeys. Establishing a consistent way of dealing with this issue is an important task. Another issue appears to be the use of tolls. It has been argued that where setting up tolls is feasible, the financial costs will be much lower. But, in a CBA context, they are a transfer from the private to the public sector; this should not affect the overall balance of costs and benefits, but will make such projects seem more affordable – for example in negotiations with the Ministry of Finance.

One positive aspect of the use of CBA is transparency: at least in the case of the Ministry of Transport, its cost-benefit assessment model is available on its website, and the CBA reports themselves are generally made public.

It is important to develop coherent and consistent use of CBA more generally in transport policy. Improvements to the rail network, through increasing capacity by doubling currently single-line tracks on long-distance routes, are ongoing, and even the construction of high speed lines is sometimes considered. This is despite the fact that passenger fares currently cover only a small fraction of operating costs, but is partly due to the fact that rail transport has a reputation of being environmentally friendly. But the geography of Norway means that long-distance rail transport is likely to be highly uneconomic compared with air transport. In the case of high-speed trains, a cost-benefit analysis carried out for Sweden showed that they could never be a cost-effective way of achieving any policy aim (OECD, 2010; Nilsson et al., 2009), while a recent report from the Swedish National Audit Office has strongly criticised a regional rail project intended to improve a region's competitiveness (Swedish National Audit Office, 2011). Generally the geography of Norway is even more unfriendly to railways than that of Sweden. Having said this, air transport is subsidised too, at least to the more remote areas. Airports in much of Norway are supported partly by cross-subsidies from the three or four airports where revenues exceed costs (such cross subsidies would probably not appear in the data in Table 1.1).

The Quality Assurance scheme for large public investment projects, a model for all CBA?

Following earlier dissatisfaction with procedures for assessing costs and benefits, a separate procedure was set up in 2005 for large public sector projects. When set up it was to apply to all projects with a likely cost of over 500 million NOK, which has now been raised to 750 million NOK (about EUR 100 million, or around 0.04% of mainland GDP). This procedure combines the features of good RIA and cost benefit analysis. It is supposed to be brought in early in the policy planning process and should analyse at least two alternative means of achieving the same objectives (to be proposed by the sponsoring ministry) plus the option of doing nothing.

The quality assurance scheme is a two-stage procedure, with the second stage assessing in more detail the expected costs and benefits of the preferred option chosen after stage 1. One of the key aspects of the process is that it is delegated to outside consultants, not carried out by the Ministry of Finance itself. It is hard to assess the results of the quality assurance scheme. Of around 30 projects that have been assessed, two were entirely rejected, including a project to host the Winter Olympic Games. A scheme that had been presented as a flagship national project, the full scale carbon capture and storage system at the Mongstad refinery, is currently in abeyance, having a large estimated excess of costs over the net present value of the benefits (despite the relatively low 2% real discount rate used). The 2010 *Economic Survey* of Norway had suggested that this project would only be viable if possible gains to the rest of the world were included in its benefits.

The fact that politically prestigious projects have been cancelled or postponed suggests that the procedure has at least some strength. In at least one case, that of a complex rail and road scheme around Oslo, it seems that projects rejected by the scheme can resurface under other headings perhaps subdivided so as to come under the 750 million NOK threshold. Overall, however, the process seems very valuable, raising the question as to whether it should be more widely used.

One problem with the idea of using the quality assurance scheme as a model is that the process in itself is quite time consuming and expensive, so is probably not suitable as a routine approach to public expenditure. A more viable alternative might be a process whereby routine CBA in ministries is subject to a "random" auditing process by an "efficiency" unit specifically charged with this task. Such a unit would have the power to investigate where it thought necessary, but would favour a small number of in-depth inquiries in areas thought to be vulnerable to poor or biased assessment. It should not have the power to overturn policy decisions that appear to be based on poor CBA – political priorities need not be subordinated to CBA, but should be required to make a reasoned case when its conclusions are overruled. Such a unit could be located in Difi, the specialised agency of the Ministry of Government, Reform and Church Affairs, or in the Ministry of Finance, and would likely also make use of outside consultants, but would need to have sufficient political backing for its reports on specific projects to have an impact on more general use of CBA.

Overall analysis of public spending

The National Audit Office

The National Audit Office, reporting to parliament, plays an important role in monitoring the implementation of government policy. With about 500 employees, it is in fact larger than the Ministry of Finance (about 300 employees). Most of its activity is necessary financial auditing, where the outcome of expenditure decisions is not its concern. But it does allocate about a quarter of its staff to "performance audits" where a key concern is whether policy goals are achieved. Such reports are potentially quite powerful; if they contain recommendations as to what ministries ought to do, and if they are approved by parliament, then ministries would have to implement the suggestions.

By its nature the Audit Office is limited to assessing goals against the aims of parliamentary legislation; it cannot evaluate those goals themselves nor compare the costs of meeting them with those under some alternative policy. The Audit Office does note, however, that in many areas efficiency could be improved with better cross-ministry co-ordination in areas such as procurement, IT systems and environmental issues. Generally speaking, only the Ministry of Finance takes a cross-cutting approach to policy, but it is more focused on keeping overall costs down that cost-efficiency *per se*.

It makes sense that the Audit Office, reporting to parliament, should not have the task of questioning parliament's decisions in its remit. For one thing, this would jeopardise the parliamentary support it needs to carry out its activities. If parliament were convinced of the need for an "efficiency" unit similar to that suggested, an important role of the audit office could be to add the necessary backing to that unit by checking that it was carrying out its mandated task.

Public spending reviews

One way of filling the gap in overall assessment of spending efficiency, and more generally in efficiency of policy choices, is a programme of spending reviews. Such reviews could follow a regular pattern of assessing policy objectives and outcomes, but also evaluating them against alternative ways of aiming at those objectives. As suggested in an OECD review of public spending in Denmark (OECD, 2012), part of the process could be to propose how 10% (or some other pre-determined percentage) cuts in resources used could be achieved at minimum loss to the objectives. This suggestion mirrors the current annual budgeting procedure, with its requirement for suggesting 4% resource savings and which have not been very effective. However, a spending review unit would be independent of individual ministries, with an independent chairperson and would include independent experts.

Currently Norway sets up *ad hoc* committees for investigating specific policy issues, whose structures are not dissimilar from that of a spending review unit. A recent one was on the disability benefit system, though it did not propose very deep reforms. A spending review process should be more systematic, though there is more than one model; in Britain such reviews are undertaken periodically in line with updating expenditure limits, in the Netherlands they are done in the year before elections. The system should aim to cover all the main spending programmes, though a rolling programme would be advisable to enable each one to be done with sufficient care.

> **Box 1.1. Recommendations on value for money in public spending**
>
> - Establish a rolling programme of independent "spending reviews" – evidence-based assessment of specific policies or programmes – as a counterpart to internal assessment. A unit to support them could be located in the Ministry of Finance but the chair should be independent and with the power to recruit key outside experts.
>
> - Improve the ability to measure outcomes against expenditure by increasing the extent to which the information in StatRes corresponds to outcome indicators used to assess performance in ministries; to maintain transparency, ensure ease of access to this information.
>
> - For cross-cutting issues, regional policy and environmental policy for example, place more emphasis on publishing estimates of overall spending, including implicit spending through methods such as market price support and cross-subsidisation, and assessing this overall spending against policy objectives.
>
> - Explore the possibility of greater use of private-sector out-sourcing in provision of local and central government services and investment where this can have beneficial effects on cost-efficiency.
>
> - Explore the potential utility of performance-based incentives for government workers to increase efficiency. In particular, evaluate whether the experiment in education management in Oslo municipality has brought efficiency gains.
>
> - Overhaul the implementation of Regulatory and Environmental Impact Assessment, cost-benefit analysis and other policy assessment tools so that they are used consistently across ministries.
>
> - Establish an "efficiency" unit, with the responsibility of auditing the use of these assessment tools to ensure this consistency, and publish the unit's reports. Such a unit could be in the Ministry of Government Administration, or the Finance Ministry, but should be established so as to be subject to performance auditing by the National Audit Office.
>
> - Require a reasoned justification for decisions which do not respect the conclusions of cost-benefit analyses.
>
> - Consider the introduction of an "efficiency dividend" system in which mandatory across-the-board cuts in ministerial budgetary allocations are redistributed annually to priority areas.
>
> - Assess the pros and cons of adopting multi-year budgeting, for example in which spending ceilings for the main spending lines in each ministry are fixed for the next three years, consistent with expected returns on the GPFG and other revenues.

Notes

1. According to the municipality of Bergen, the second largest in Norway.
2. Switching resources from agricultural market price support to wage subsidies, for example, could be done by reducing guaranteed prices to farmers while increasing taxes on food by an equivalent

amount so average food prices to the consumer were unchanged, using the resulting revenue for wage subsidies. The fact that this might increase apparent levels of taxation, against government policy, is a reflection of the hidden taxation inherent in market price support.

Bibliography

Boarini, R. (2009), "Making the most of Norwegian schools", *OECD Economics Department Working Papers*, No. 661.

Bonnesrønning, H., L.E. Borge, M. Haraldsvik and B. Strøm (2008), "Ressurser og resultater i grunnopplaeringen: Forsprosjekt", Centre for Economic Research at NTNU, SØF Report No. 03/08.

Calmfors, L. (2010), "Lessons from Sweden", paper presented at the Conference on Independent Fiscal Institutions, Budapest, 18-19 March.

Edvardsen, D.F., F.R. Forund and S.A. Kittelsen (2010), "Effektivitets- og produktivitetsanalyser på StatRes-data", Ragnar Frisch Centre for Economic Research, Report 2/2010.

EPSI (2010), Nordmenns tilfredshet med offentlige tjenester, 2010 (Nordic people's satisfaction with public services), EPSI (Extended Performance Satisfaction Index), Norway, www.epsi-norway.org/images/stories/reports/Scanning/Presseinformasjon_offentlige_tjenester_2010.pdf.

Erlandsen, E. (2008), "Improving the efficiency of health care spending: what can be learnt from partial and selected analysis of hospital performance", *OECD Economic Studies*, No. 44, Vol. 1.

Eriksen, K., H. Minken, G. Steenberg, T. Sunde and K.-E. Hagen (2007), "Evaluering av OPS i vegsektoren" ("Evaluation of PPP in the road sector"), Institute of Transport Economics, Oslo, Report 890/2007.

Hagemann, R. (2010), "Improving fiscal performance through fiscal councils", *OECD Economics Department Working Paper*, No. 829.

House of Commons (2011), Parliamentary Select Committee on the Treasury, Report on the Private Finance Initiative.

Irish Ministry of Finance (2011), "Reforming Ireland's Budgetary Framework: A Discussion Document," March.

Joumard, I., C. André and C. Nicq (2010), "Health Care Systems: Efficiency and Institutions", *OECD Economics Department Working Papers*, No. 769, OECD Publishing, http://dx.doi.org/10.1787/5kmfp51f5f9t-en.

Loegreid P., P.G. Roness and K. Rubecksen (2005), "Performance management in practice – the Norwegian way", paper presented to EGPA conference, Bern, 31 August-3 September, 2005 http://soc.kuleuven.be/io/cost/pub/paper/EGPABern22.pdf.

Ministry of Education (2009), "Analyse av kostnader i barnehagene i 2008", August, www.regjeringen.no/upload/KD/Vedlegg/Barnehager/Rapporter%20og%20planer/Analyse%20av%20kostnader%20i%20barnehagen%20i%202008.pdf.

Ministry of Finance (2010), State Budget, 2011, Annex 1: Background material for the proposed budget for the program category 13.50 District and Regional Policy, www.statsbudsjettet.no/Statsbudsjettet-2011/Dokumenter/Fagdepartementenes-proposisjoner/Kommunal-og-regionaldepartementet-KRD/Prop-1-S/48148/48149/.

Nilsson, J.E. and R. Pydokke (2009), "High-speed Railways – a Climate Policy Sidetrack" (summary in English), Swedish National Road and Transport Research Institute, Report to the Expert Group on Environmental Studies, Swedish Ministry of Finance.

OECD (2005), *OECD Economic Survey of Norway 2005*, OECD Publishing, Paris.

OECD (2007), *OECD Territorial Reviews: Norway*, OECD Publishing, Paris.

OECD (2008), *OECD Economic Survey of Norway, 2008*, OECD Publishing, Paris.

OECD (2010), *OECD Economic Survey of Norway, 2010*, OECD Publishing, Paris.

OECD (2011a), *OECD Reviews of Evaluation and Assessment in Education: Norway*, OECD Publishing, Paris.

OECD (2011b), *Government at a Glance*, OECD Publishing, Paris.

OECD (2012), *Value for Money in Government, Denmark 2011*, OECD Publishing, Paris.

Swedish National Audit Office (2011), "The Bothnia Line and the railway along the Norrland coast" (RiR 2011:22).

Chapter 2

Tax reform in Norway: A focus on capital taxation

> *Norway's dual income tax system achieves high levels of revenue collection and income redistribution, without overly undermining economic performance and while paying attention to environmental externalities. It treats capital and labour income in different ways: capital income is taxed at a single low rate, while labour income is taxed at progressive rates. However, effective tax rates on savings vary widely across asset classes. The favourable treatment of owner-occupied housing relative to financial savings should be reduced, preferably by taxing imputed rents at the standard 28% statutory rate. The wealth tax implies very high effective tax rates on savings, indicating that it either gives rise to tax avoidance or significantly inhibits growth. The government should investigate the issue and, if the growth-equity trade-off is too unfavourable to growth, phase out or lower the wealth tax. To restrain tax avoidance by the wealthy, the base of the gift and inheritance tax should be broadened. Overall, the reform package recommended in this chapter would improve the allocation of capital and increase work and investment incentives. It could be designed to be broadly neutral in regard to income redistribution and public revenue.*

Because of high spending, Norway needs to collect large amounts of tax revenue. This results in a higher mainland tax-to-GDP ratio than in almost any other OECD country (Figure 2.1 and Box 2.1). The high level of taxation does not appear to overly undermine economic growth, as witnessed by the impressive performance of the economy, and it allows for considerable income redistribution, which facilitates the prevalence of an egalitarian society (see Figure 1). This suggests that the tax system is generally designed in an efficient way – in the sense of attaining high social welfare in terms of both average incomes and equity considerations. Norway's tax system nonetheless displays a number of deficiencies, mainly in the capital part of the tax system. The chapter therefore focuses on this area. It provides an analysis of all types of capital taxation: personal income taxation of the return to savings, corporate income taxation, wealth taxation, local property taxation, the stamp duty on property transactions and gift and inheritance taxation. For the mainland economy in 2008, these taxes amounted to NOK 118 billion, or 14% of the overall tax revenue of the government. The implied economic distortions could be larger than this might suggest.

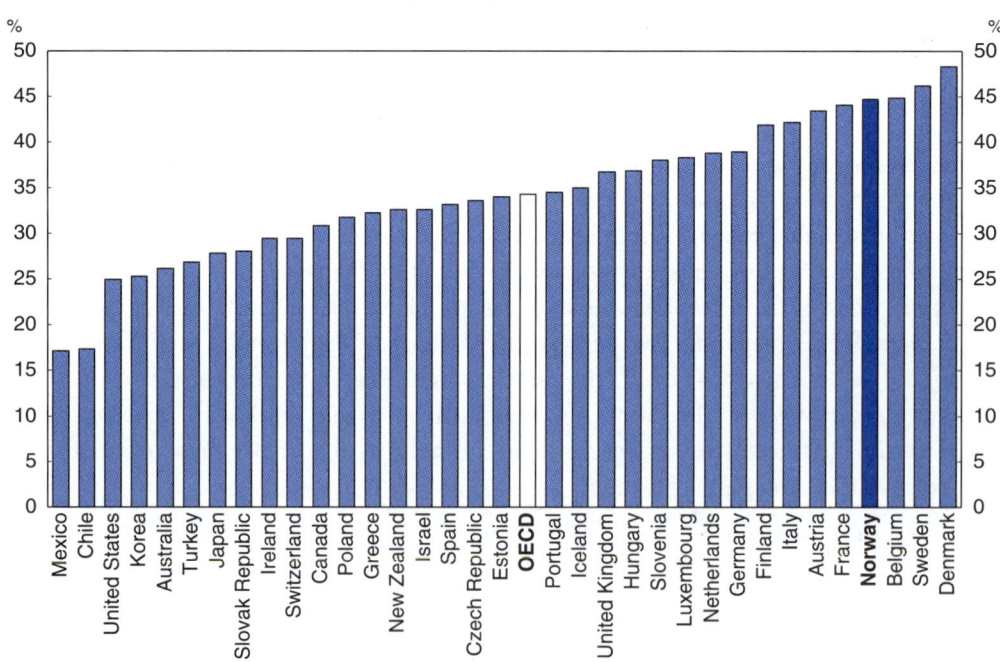

Figure 2.1. **Government tax receipts**[1]
As a percentage of GDP, 2010[2]

Note: Data for Norway refer to mainland. OECD area is the simple average of OECD countries for which data are available.
1. Include social security contributions, total direct taxes on households and businesses, taxes on production and imports; and exclude capital tax and transfer receipts.
2. Or latest year available.
Source: OECD Economic Outlook Database.

StatLink ⟶ http://dx.doi.org/10.1787/888932572330

> **Box 2.1. Main characteristics of the Norwegian tax system**
>
> As other OECD countries, Norway relies to a large extent on personal income taxation (i.e. labour income taxation and capital income taxation), consumption taxation and corporate income taxation to raise public revenue. The level of each of these three tax categories is significantly above its respective average in the OECD (Table 2.1):
>
> - Personal income taxation (as a share of mainland GDP) is the fourth highest in the OECD. Statutory personal income tax rates are flat relative to the tax base in OECD-wide comparison (Joumard, Pisu and Bloch, 2012). Ordinary income, defined as the sum of labour and capital income, above the personal allowance of NOK 45 350 per year, is taxed at 28%. Capital income in the form of dividends and capital gains is tax-exempt up to the "normal" (or risk-free) return. Surtaxes of 9% and 12%, respectively, are levied on labour income exceeding NOK 490 000 and NOK 796 400 per year. The standard employers' and employees' social security contribution rates are 14.1% and 7.8%. Employers' social security contributions are charged at a reduced rate in less populated areas.
>
> - Consumption taxation (as a share of mainland GDP) is the third highest in the OECD, primarily because the 25% standard rate of the value-added tax is well above the OECD average of 19%. The consumption of foodstuffs is taxed at the reduced rate of 15% (up from 14% in 2011), and the supply and procurement of passenger transport as well as the letting of hotel rooms and holiday homes are taxed at 8%.
>
> - Corporate income taxation (as a share of total GDP) is by some margin the highest in the OECD, mainly thanks to the large tax payments by petroleum companies. The standard statutory tax rate is 28%, and special taxes of 50% and 30% are imposed on the income from petroleum extraction and hydro power, respectively.
>
> *Note:* The levels of statutory tax rates and allowances are those proposed for 2012 in Ministry of Finance (2011a).
>
> **Table 2.1. Tax revenue by main tax category, 2010**
> As a percentage of GDP
>
> | Selected OECD countries | Personal income | Consumption | Corporate income |
> | --- | --- | --- | --- |
> | **Norway** | 25.7 | 15.4 | 9.7 |
> | Sweden | 27.6 | 13.5 | 3.5 |
> | Finland | 25.1 | 13.3 | 2.5 |
> | Denmark | 27.9 | 15.2 | 2.7 |
> | Germany | 23.1 | 10.7 | 1.5 |
> | France | 25.3 | 10.7 | 2.1 |
> | Italy | 24.8 | 11.0 | 2.8 |
> | United Kingdom | 16.7 | 10.8 | 3.1 |
> | United States | 14.4 | 4.4 | 2.7 |
> | Canada | 16.9 | 7.7 | 3.4 |
> | Japan | 16.5 | 5.2 | 2.6 |
> | Korea | 9.4 | 8.5 | 3.5 |
> | **OECD average** | **18.1** | **11.0** | **2.9** |
>
> *Note:* For Norway, data on personal income and consumption refer to the mainland and on corporate income to the total economy.
> *Source:* OECD, *Revenue Statistics Database* and *OECD Economic Outlook Database*.

Main features of the dual income tax system

Norway, like Denmark, Finland and Sweden, has a dual income tax system which differentiates taxation depending on the source of income, with capital income taxed differently to non-capital (mainly labour) income. The sum of labour income and capital income (referred to as ordinary income) is taxed at a statutory rate of 28%. Labour income is subject to additional taxation stemming from social security contributions and surtaxes levied above certain thresholds. This approach seeks to limit the type of distortion induced by the traditional comprehensive income tax system, which taxes labour income and capital income in the same way and results in double taxation of earned labour income and high tax rates on real returns. Dual income taxation has gained broad support in many European countries. The German corporate tax reform of 2008, for example, abandoned the previous comprehensive income tax in favour of a dual income tax-like system.

Dual income taxation is based on the principles of: i) broad tax bases; ii) progressive labour income tax rates; and iii) a small proportional (i.e. below the tax rates on labour income) statutory tax rate on capital income. These characteristics are generally seen to be conducive to efficiency (see e.g. Griffith, Hines and Sørensen, 2010). Broad tax bases reduce marginal rates and hence deadweight losses. Levying a statutory rate on capital income below that on labour income takes, up to a degree, into account the double taxation of labour income and the taxation of purely inflationary gains. It promotes savings, investment and thus growth (the more so, the larger is the home bias in investment). In the face of high capital mobility, it also reduces the incentive of residents to hide their assets abroad. Proportional (as opposed to progressive) taxation of capital income eliminates the arbitrage opportunities that would arise if people were subject to different marginal capital income tax rates.

With respect to equity considerations, progressive labour income taxation contributes to income redistribution. While the taxation of capital income is proportional relative to its base, the highly skewed distribution of financial capital (Figure 2.2) implies that the richest 10% of households pay approximately 70% of all tax revenue from capital income. Even proportional taxation of capital income thus ensures a relatively large contribution of these households to the financing of social transfers which in turn helps to narrow income inequality.

Under certain assumptions, a reasonable case can be made that, in principle, capital income should be subject to zero taxation. A key reason is to avoid saving out of current income being double taxed – once when labour income is earned and again when the return on savings is earned. Double taxation of savings would result in future consumption being taxed more heavily than current consumption, thus inducing a distortion. This is what motivated the authors of the *Mirrlees Review* (2011) of taxation in the United Kingdom to advocate full exemption of the "normal" (or risk-free) return to savings from taxation. As Box 2.2 argues in some more detail, the design of the system of capital taxation is therefore important from the perspective of both efficiency and growth. It influences the investment incentives, the allocation of savings and the degree of intergenerational mobility in the economy.

A number of arguments, however, both theoretical and practical, can be advanced to justify non-zero taxation of capital income. For instance, people with high earnings ability and hence high ability to pay taxes may have a higher propensity to save (for evidence, see the studies cited in Banks and Diamond, 2010) or be better at achieving a higher

Figure 2.2. **Average taxable gross financial capital per household, 2009**

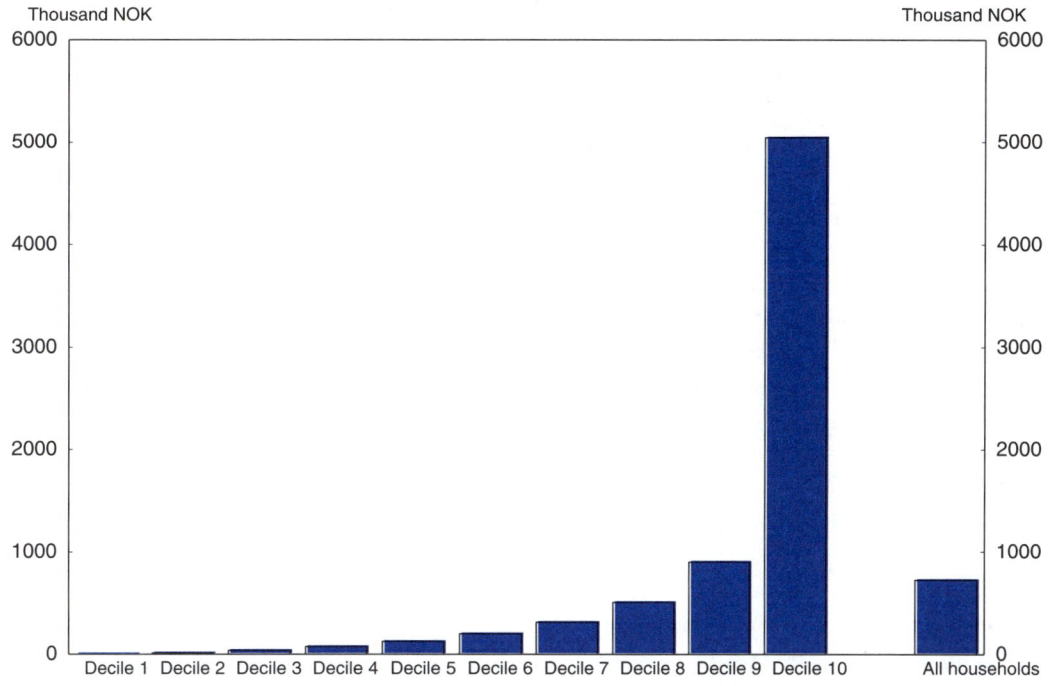

Note: Students are not included.
Source: Statistics Norway.

StatLink ᘎᔕᒕ http://dx.doi.org/10.1787/888932572349

> Box 2.2. **Why the design of capital taxation matters for efficiency and growth**
>
> The design of the system of capital taxation is important from the perspective of both efficiency and growth:
>
> ● Academic arguments against capital taxation usually draw on two seminal studies (for an overview, see *e.g.* Salanie, 2003; Mankiw, Weinzierl and Yagan, 2009; Diamond and Saez, 2011). Firstly, the compounding of the tax burden on savings and wealth through time may drive an increasing wedge between the pre- and post-tax return to capital, reducing the capital stock and aggregate output in the long run (Judd, 1985; Chamley, 1986). Secondly, capital taxes represent double taxation of labour income which had already been taxed when earned and hence distort the intertemporal decision of a person when to spend her income but have no beneficial effect on her incentives to supply labour (Atkinson and Stiglitz, 1976).
>
> ● However, as discussed in the main text and footnote 1, some taxation of real capital income can be justified. On the other hand, if capital taxes are set too high, they are likely to overly reduce the level of savings in the economy; for numerical simulations based on a standard life-cycle model, see *e.g.* Attanasio and Wakefield (2010). In a fully open economy, the size of domestic savings would be largely irrelevant for domestic investment and growth, but arguably no economy can be described as fully open in this sense. Between 2006 and 2009, Norwegian investors on average accounted for 46% of the market value of the Oslo Stock Exchange (Södersten and Lindhe, 2011).

> **Box 2.2. Why the design of capital taxation matters for efficiency and growth** *(cont.)*
>
> - In a relatively open economy like Norway, the corporate income tax system that is faced by all investors is likely a more important determinant of investment and growth than the capital income tax at the personal level that applies only to residents. Hines (1999) and Devereux and Griffith (2002) provide summaries of the relevant empirical literature, concluding that the international location of real investment is indeed sensitive to tax policies. Differences in the relative tax treatment of asset classes (interest-bearing accounts, shares, housing, etc.) change their relative rates of return and thus potentially the form of investment undertaken. Taxing capital may also indirectly reduce labour supply (depending on the size of the substitution and the income effect) since higher capital taxes will reduce the value of any given labour income.
> - Capital taxation is instrumental in facilitating intergenerational mobility, another channel through which it could impact efficiency and growth. This is most obvious in the case of inheritance taxation; one of the key rationales for inheritance taxation is the improvement of equality of opportunity (for a summary, see *e.g.* Kopczuk, 2009; Boadway, Chamberlain and Emmerson, 2010).

(average) rate of return on financial investments. Taxing capital income is also useful to reduce incentives for tax arbitrage or evasion, for example small business owners reporting their labour income as capital income or self-employed individuals incorporating solely for tax purposes; a practice found in some countries with low capital income tax rates.[1]

The taxation of capital can be broadly divided into the taxation of the *income* from capital, the taxation of the *stock* of capital and the taxation of the *transfer* of capital. In Norway, the taxation of capital income includes personal income taxation (of interest, dividends, rents, capital gains) and corporate income taxation. The stock of capital is taxed through the wealth tax and the local property tax, while capital transfers are subject to the stamp duty and the gift and inheritance tax. Figure 2.3 shows the relative importance of these six categories in the mainland revenue from capital taxation. Corporate and personal income taxes make up, respectively, 55% and 22%, while revenues from wealth, local property, stamp duty, gifts and inheritances together account for 22%.

Table 2.2 summarises the key features of these different categories of capital taxation. In principle, all nominal returns to savings (interest, dividends, rents, capital gains) and all corporate profits are subject to a flat 28% statutory tax rate. However, a number of exemptions exist, chief among them are imputed incomes and capital gains from owner-occupied housing. Surtaxes also prevail, for instance citizens with wealth above NOK 750 000 (approximately EUR 100 000) face an annual tax of 1.1% on their wealth in excess of this threshold.[2] At the moment, 17% of the adult population pay the wealth tax. The wealth tax is not applied at the same rate across asset classes because real estate and individual private (IPS) pensions are treated favourably. Finally, a stamp duty of 2.5% applies to the transaction price of a property, and taxes of 6% and 10% are imposed on gifts and inheritances to children, above certain thresholds.

A traditional, but ill-conceived argument in favour of wealth taxes is that they tax a separate base. In fact, taxes on capital income and taxes on the capital stock are largely identical. Consider a citizen with wealth of NOK 100 million that earns a rate of return of 4% or a return of NOK 4 million. It is irrelevant whether the government levies a tax

Figure 2.3. **Mainland revenue from capital taxation, 2008**

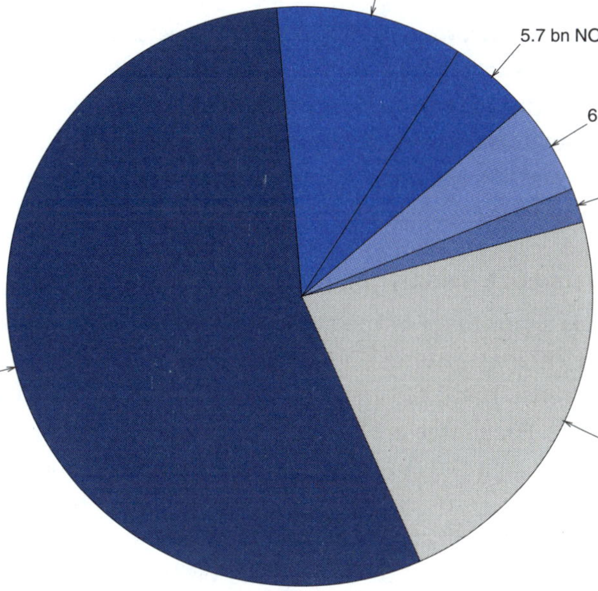

- 11.9 bn NOK, Wealth taxation
- 5.7 bn NOK, Local property taxation
- 6.1 bn NOK, Stamp duty
- 2.3 bn NOK, Gifts and inheritance taxation
- 65.2 bn NOK, Corporate income taxation (mainland)
- 26.4 bn NOK, Personal income taxation

Source: Ministry of Finance and Statistics Norway.

StatLink ⟶ http://dx.doi.org/10.1787/888932572368

Table 2.2. **Categories of capital taxation**

	Statutory tax rates	Supplementary notes
Taxation of capital income:		
Personal income taxation	28%	Full exemption on imputed incomes and capital gains from owner-occupied housing; effective reduction on individual private (IPS) pensions; rate of return allowance on dividends and capital gains
Corporate income taxation	28%	50% additional tax on petroleum companies
Taxation of the capital stock:		
Wealth taxation	1.1% annually on wealth in excess of NOK 750 000	Reductions on owner-occupied housing and rental housing; full exemption on IPS pensions
Local property taxation	0-0.7% annually on the property value	Set by the municipalities; not used by one third of them
Taxation of capital transfers:		
Stamp duty	2.5% on the transaction price	Full exemption on co-operatives
Gift and inheritance taxation	6% (10%) on gifts and inheritances received during life in excess of NOK 470 000 (800 000), calculated separately for each donor	Annual allowances; tax rates for beneficiaries other than children are higher but apply only to inheritances, not gifts

of 28% on the capital income of NOK 4 million (= NOK 1.1 million) or a wealth tax of 1.1% on the capital stock of NOK 100 million (= NOK 1.1 million). It follows that a capital income tax of 28% *or* a wealth tax of 1.1% yields the same tax burden (when the rate of return is 4%). Imposing on a person a capital income tax of 28% *and* a wealth tax of 1.1% then means that she effectively pays twice as much tax as the rate of the capital income tax alone suggests. (This is numerically confirmed in Table 2.4 below.) The chapter therefore considers wealth taxation as a form of capital income taxation.

The taxation of capital income and wealth

As shown in Table 2.2, incomes from different asset classes are treated differently by the tax system, with some left largely untaxed, while others are subject to surtaxes. It is hard to find a compelling economic argument that may justify the preferential tax treatment of some asset classes over others.[3] A tax system that is neutral with respect to the type of assets owned avoids encouraging investment in what would otherwise be unproductive uses (Arnold et al., 2011; *Mirrlees Review*, 2011; Jacobs, 2011).

Investments in housing are heavily favoured by the tax system

Table 2.3 provides a summary of the statutory tax treatment of five asset classes that are available to most citizens: interest-bearing accounts, shares, housing (separately for owner-occupied and rental) and IPS pensions. The nominal return on interest-bearing accounts is taxed at 28%. For shares in Norwegian companies, taxation occurs at two levels; at the corporate level through the corporate income tax and at the personal level through the personal income tax. The corporate income tax rate is flat at 28%. On the remaining 72%, an additional 28% is levied on dividends and capital gains if their rate of return exceeds the normal rate of return (defined as the average interest rate on three-month Treasury bills). This implies a total tax for shares of 28% on the normal return and 48% (= 28% + 28% * 72%) on above-normal returns. No tax applies to the returns on owner-occupied housing, while rents and capital gains from rental housing are subject to the standard 28% tax rate.[4] Mortgage interest on both owner-occupied and rental housing is fully deductible. For pensions, the focus in this chapter is on the voluntary IPS scheme, because savings in the National Insurance and occupational schemes are mandatory and therefore not substitutable with other investment vehicles. The IPS scheme does not tax capital incomes directly, but in most cases these are indirectly brought into the tax base through the taxation of pension income at the point of withdrawal.

Table 2.3. **Tax treatment of asset classes**

Asset class	Capital income taxation	Wealth taxation (in excess of NOK 750 000)
Interest-bearing accounts:	28% personal income tax on the nominal return	1.1%
Shares:	28% corporate income tax on nominal profits; in addition, 28% personal income tax on dividends and capital gains in excess of the normal return	1.1%
Housing:		
Owner-occupied housing	0%	Effectively 0.275% (valued 25% in the tax base)
Rental housing	28% personal income tax on rents and capital gains	Effectively 0.44% (valued 40% in the tax base)
Individual private (IPS) pensions:	0% during accumulation (effectively above 0% through the taxation of pension income at withdrawal)	0%

In addition to the taxation of capital income, a wealth tax of 1.1% per year is imposed on the capital stock above NOK 750 000. The valuation in the base of the wealth tax varies enormously across asset classes. On one end interest-bearing accounts and shares are valued at 100%, while on the other IPS pensions are completely exempt. Owner-occupied and rental housing are treated favourably because only a portion of their value is included in the tax base (25% and 40%, respectively), which is equivalent to wealth tax rates of 0.275% (= 25% * 1.1%) and 0.44% (= 40% * 1.1%) respectively.

Hence, the tax system treats asset classes in different ways. To transparently capture the total tax liability due on each asset class, it is useful to subsume all the taxes applying to any one asset into a single one. To this end, Table 2.4 provides for each class the effective tax rate (ETR), defined as the percentage reduction in the annual real rate of return on an extra NOK of saving caused by the tax system:

$$ETR = \frac{(\text{pre tax real rate of return}) - (\text{post tax real rate of return})}{\text{pre tax real rate of return}}.$$

If no tax on capital is levied, then the post-tax real rate of return will equal the pre-tax real rate of return, and the ETR will be 0%. By contrast, if the entire real return is taxed away, then the post-tax real rate of return will be 0%, which implies an ETR of 100%. The calculations are done separately for individuals who pay and those who do not pay the wealth tax. Annex 2.A1 explains them in detail. The underlying assumptions are a pre-tax nominal rate of return of 4% and an inflation rate of 2%. These correspond closely to the nominal rate of return to government bonds and consumer price inflation in Norway since 2000. The ETRs are the effective tax rates prescribed by law. To the extent that people avoid or evade paying capital income or wealth taxes, the actual effective tax rates that they pay could be lower.

Table 2.4. **Effective tax rates on the real income from different assets**

	Without wealth tax (%)	With wealth tax (%)
Interest-bearing accounts	56	113
Shares	56	113
Owner-occupied housing	0	14
Rental housing	56	79
Individual private (IPS) pensions	37	37

Note: The calculations are done for a nominal rate of return of 4% and an inflation rate of 2%, which correspond closely to the nominal rate of return to government bonds and consumer price inflation in Norway since 2000. The effective tax rates (ETRs) apply to an extra NOK of saving by a Norwegian resident investing in a Norwegian asset. The ETRs for shares are based on nominal depreciation rates which are a reasonable approximation to how the Norwegian tax system functions as tax depreciation depends on the cost price (and not the repurchase price) and the expected life span of the asset. The ETRs for owner-occupied housing and rental housing are independent of the degree of debt finance versus self-finance when assuming that mortgage interest rates equal savings interest rates. The ETRs for IPS pensions are based on a tax rate on pension income of 39% and the assumption that the initial savings stay in the scheme for 15 years and are then paid out over a period of 15 years (as an annuity).
Source: Ministry of Finance.

The table illustrates the serious shortcomings of the current system in aligning tax rates across all asset classes and maintaining an ETR on capital income not above the tax rates on labour income. (The top labour income tax rate, including social security contributions, is 54%.) For people not paying the wealth tax, owner-occupied housing and IPS pension investments enjoy generous tax advantages. The statutory capital income tax rate of 28% applies in full only to the income from interest-bearing accounts, shares and rental housing, resulting in an ETR of 56%. Intuitively, since the tax system applies the statutory rate to the nominal return, the ETR on the real return, when the real return is half the nominal return, is twice the statutory rate (56% = 2 * 28%).

The wealth tax doubles the ETR on interest-bearing accounts and shares. Intuitively, the wealth tax knocks 1.1% off the stock which is more than half the real return of 2%, and thus adds more than 50% to the ETR on interest-bearing accounts and shares. The wealth tax amplifies the preferential treatment of housing, due to its undervaluation in the tax base. As a result, for persons paying the wealth tax, the ETR on interest-bearing accounts and shares (113%) is 8 times that on owner-occupied housing (14%), 3 times that on IPS pensions (37%) and 1.5 times that on rental housing (79%). That more than 50% of household wealth is held in housing property and more than 80% of household debt accounted for by mortgages (Figure 2.4) suggest that the implicit tax subsidies to housing investments influence the savings decisions of households.

Figure 2.4. **Household wealth and debt, second quarter 2009**

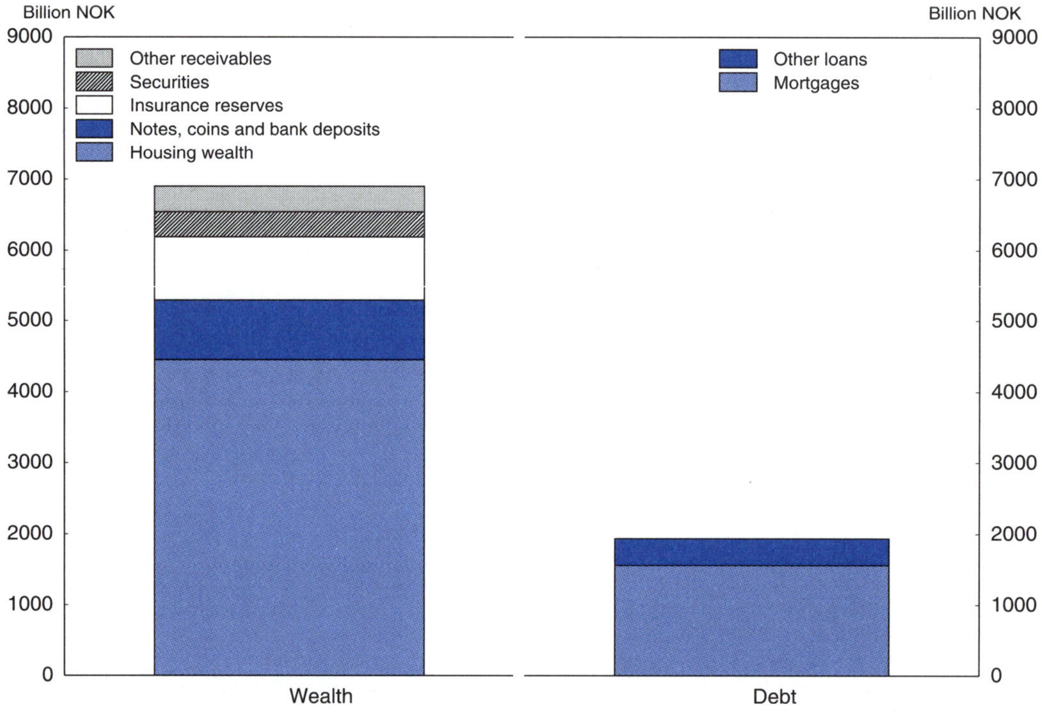

Source: Statistics Norway and Norges Bank.

StatLink http://dx.doi.org/10.1787/888932572387

The taxation of imputed rents should be re-introduced, at the level of alternative types of investments

Neutrality of investment stipulates that the ETR should be the same across asset classes. For owner-occupied housing, this could be achieved through the introduction of the taxation of imputed rents and capital gains at the statutory tax rate of 28% that applies to alternative types of investments.[5] Imputed rents represent the rental income that an owner-occupying household would receive if it rented the property to a different household. They should therefore be taxed. Possible external benefits from owner occupation, in so far as any exist, cannot plausibly justify the currently extraordinarily preferential treatment. Norway used to tax the returns to owner occupation until 2005. Political considerations were the major driving force behind the abolition of the tax. But the tax was generally not very effective because the tax-assessed values were quite random and particularly low (relative to the market values) for expensive houses.

Rather than property values as in the previous system, the tax base in a reformed system should preferably be imputed rents. From a political perspective, contrary to a tax on imputed rents (whose rate should be the same 28% that applies to interest, dividends, rents and capital gains), setting the tax rate on property values would likely be more subjective. From an economic perspective, property values are only an imprecise measure of the returns to housing, since, unless future rents are expected to change similarly in all geographical areas, the distribution of house prices will differ from the distribution of imputed rents across areas. In most areas, the rental market should be sufficiently large to allow for a reliable estimation of the unobserved rents on owner-occupied housing. Elsewhere, house prices and average price-to-rent ratios could be used as an indirect means to estimate imputed rents. The levels of imputed rents should then be updated regularly. The aim should be a *gradual* introduction of imputed rent taxation to minimise the economic impact on current owners who would suffer windfall losses as a result of the reform. If taxation of (imputed) rents and capital gains from owner-occupied and rental housing is implemented, full deductibility of mortgage interest and other expenses should be retained.

An alternative is to assume that imputed rents are proportional to property values and introduce a housing property tax at the national level. This tax would use the property valuation system that is already in place for the wealth tax. The tax rate on house prices should then in principle be set so that the revenue from housing property taxation would (in aggregate) equal the revenue from the taxation of imputed rents. To bring unexpected capital gains into the tax base, the housing property tax should be accompanied by the introduction of the taxation of capital gains on owner-occupied housing at the standard capital income tax rate of 28%. If such a system of taxation of property values were applied to both owner-occupied and rental housing, the existing taxation of rents (but not capital gains) from rental housing should be discontinued, as otherwise both the return and the stock of rental housing would be taxed. In any case, full deductibility of mortgage interest and other expenses should be retained.

A final – though less desirable – possibility to reduce the preferential tax treatment of owner-occupied housing would be to eliminate mortgage interest deductibility on owner-occupied housing. This would raise the ETR on the debt-financed part of owner-occupied housing towards the 56% due on interest-bearing accounts, shares and rental housing (for households not paying the wealth tax). By contrast, the ETR on the self-financed part of owner-occupied housing would remain 0%. At the moment, the deductibility of mortgage interest ensures that the tax system leaves home buyers indifferent between debt finance and self-finance. While removing mortgage interest relief would tend to raise the average ETR on owner-occupied housing, this advantage would come at the cost of giving rise to the additional distortion of the tax system pushing households to self-finance their houses. In addition, because of the difficulties ring-fencing interest related to mortgages on owner-occupied houses, abolishing mortgage interest deductibility would probably introduce some debt shifting in the personal income tax, thereby undermining the uniform treatment of different sources of capital income.

The government should investigate the economic effects of the tax breaks to the IPS pension scheme

IPS deposits are fairly small-scale, partly explained by various restrictions; at the moment, they account for less than 0.1% of all household deposits. The biggest tax advantage of IPS pensions is their exemption from the wealth tax. However, even if IPS pensions were included in the base of the wealth tax, their ETR would be significantly lower than that on interest-bearing accounts and shares. The mandatory National Insurance and occupational schemes are meant to ensure a sufficient pension level for all citizens. In some countries, tax privileges to voluntary pension plans may be useful to allow citizens to hedge their risk of not receiving the public and private pensions that the mandatory schemes promise. This argument applies to a much lesser degree in Norway given the sheer size of its sovereign wealth. The government should investigate which individuals participate in the IPS pension scheme and the likely impact of the tax breaks on their total saving. If the results show that IPS pensions are primarily taken up by the more well-off households with no significant change to their saving, it should phase out all tax breaks to the scheme.

Taxing imputed rents and capital gains from owner occupation would align tax rates across asset classes under the capital income tax but would not remove the distortions due to the current undervaluation of owner-occupied and rental housing and business property in the base of the wealth tax. Some upward corrections to the valuation of different asset classes have been taken recently. In 2010, the valuation of housing property and business property was raised somewhat (Figure 2.5). But since the tax base now accounts for shares in full, this change in the valuation structure of the wealth tax is likely to have made the tax advantages of housing property and IPS pensions even more pronounced, plausibly giving rise to a further misallocation of capital in the economy. The government should remove the special treatment of real estate, IPS pensions and business property in the wealth tax. In this context, it was right to reject calls by the Confederation of Norwegian Enterprise (NHO), Norway's major organisation for employers, to introduce an exemption in the wealth tax on working capital. This would merely have led to an additional undermining of a system already packed with exemptions.

Effective tax rates on people paying the wealth tax are very high, sometimes exceeding 100%

If the base of the wealth tax included all assets at full value, at current rates the ETR for people paying the wealth tax would increase to 113% for all asset classes. The wealth tax implies that, contrary to the idea of dual income taxation, capital income is not taxed at a flat but highly progressive rate, with the marginal tax rate on capital income for wealthy households being in effect twice the one for less wealthy households. An ETR higher than 100% for wealth tax payers means that by saving these people actually *reduce* the real value of their wealth. The reasons for the ETR taking on levels of above 100% are twofold. The statutory tax rates apply to the nominal return and not the real return, and the wealth tax mechanically reduces wealth and hence may siphon off all (or even more than all) of the real return.

ETRs of above 100% are bound to encourage wealthy households to seek avoidance and evasion opportunities. To the extent that these ETRs are actually paid, they should be a strong disincentive to save and invest, which could be one factor to explain why mainland business investment as a share of mainland GDP is so low (for details, see Figure 2.9 below).

Figure 2.5. **Valuation in the base of the wealth tax**

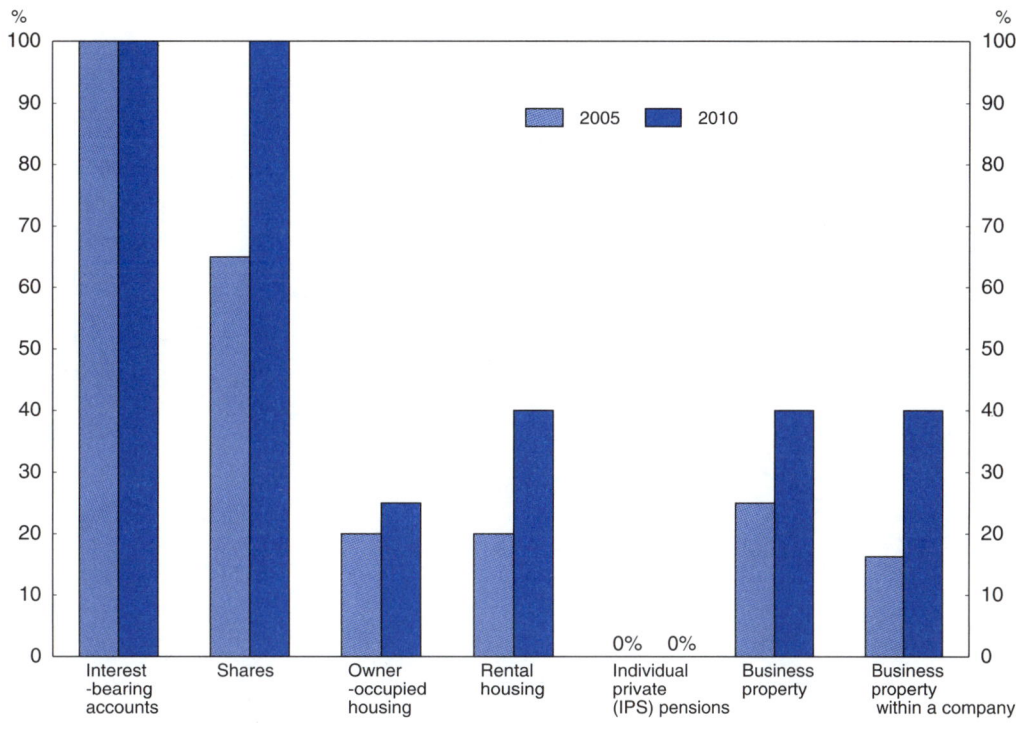

Source: Ministry of Finance.

StatLink ⇒ http://dx.doi.org/10.1787/888932572406

By significantly reducing the value of labour income, they are also likely to have an overly harmful impact on the labour supply of wealthy citizens.

Figure 2.6 illustrates these strong disincentives to work for a person in the top labour income tax bracket who must decide whether to work for an additional labour income now (say, when she is 40) which she considers spending during her old age (when she will be 70). Her labour income is subject to the top labour income tax rate of 54% (including social security contributions). If she consumed her labour income immediately, her consumption would be taxed at the (standard rate of the) value-added tax of 25%, resulting in a total tax wedge of 66% (= 54% + 25% * 46%). If she has to pay the wealth tax and wants to consume her earned labour income after 30 years instead, the total tax wedge due to the combination of capital income and wealth taxation will rise to 82%.

In a background paper to the *Mirrlees Review* (2011), Brewer, Saez and Shephard (2010) estimate the revenue-maximising (or top of the Laffer curve) tax rate on labour income (including social security contributions) and consumption for the highest earners as 56%. This is 10 percentage points below Norway's current one, although the Norway-specific revenue-maximising tax rate would likely be lower given its in comparison harsher tax treatment of capital. That this effect could be at play is borne out by evidence documenting that people with total income (*i.e.* sum of labour income and capital income) of above NOK 3 million pay less income tax (as a share of pre-tax income) than people with total income of NOK 0.75-3 million (Ministry of Finance, 2011b). People with total income of above NOK 3 million probably pay more capital income tax (as a share of pre-tax income) than people with total income of NOK 0.75-3 million. This suggests that they pay less

Figure 2.6. **Total tax wedge on deferred consumption (for labour income earned in year 0)**

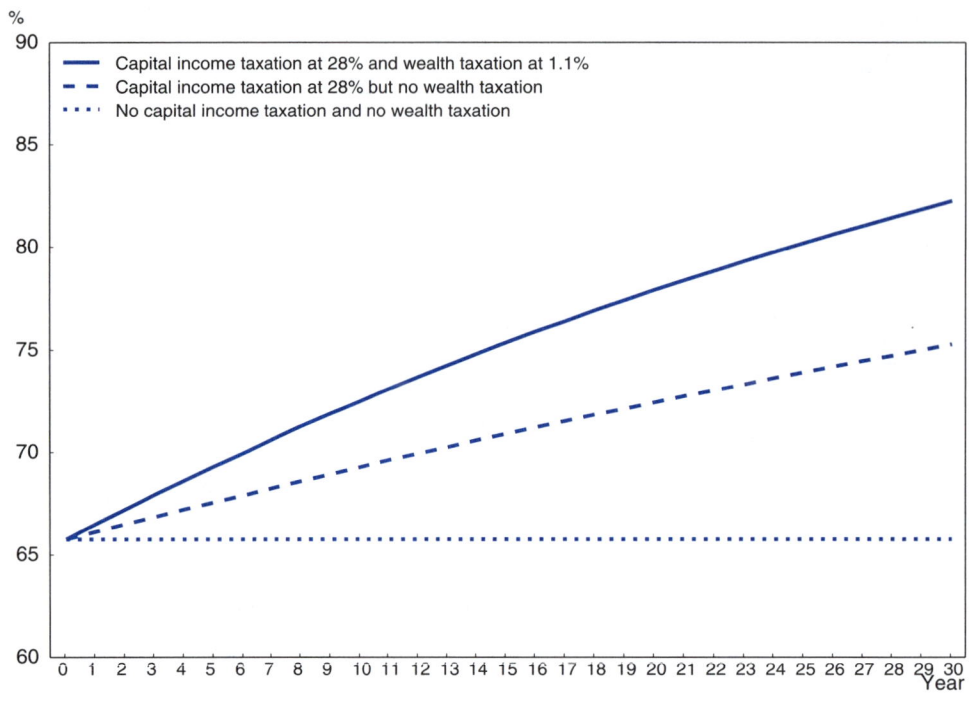

Note: The total tax wedge accounts for labour income taxation (including all social security contributions) at the top rate of 54% and consumption taxation at the standard value-added rate of 25%. With no capital income taxation and no wealth taxation the total tax wedge does not depend on when the earned labour income is spent. Capital income taxation and/or wealth taxation raise the total tax wedge – all the more, the later the labour income earned in year 0 is spent. The calculations are done for a nominal rate of return of 4% and an inflation rate of 2%. The tax rates indicated in the legend are the statutory ones.
Source: OECD Secretariat calculations.

StatLink ⟶ http://dx.doi.org/10.1787/888932572425

labour income tax and hence that labour income and labour supply may be declining for persons paying the wealth tax.

Even for a society with a very high preference for redistribution, which arguably is the case for Norway, it cannot be efficient to impose on some citizens capital income tax rates of above 100% on the real return of some assets. Following the *Mirrlees Review* (2011) of taxation in the United Kingdom, the "optimal" ETR in Table 2.4 would be 0% on all asset classes. While this view is not universally shared, ETRs on capital income above the tax rates on labour income are generally seen as not desirable. The very high ETRs could be reduced either through the wealth tax or, in principle, the capital income tax. However, any significant cut in the capital income tax rate would lower its statutory rate below the one on labour income, encouraging individuals to declare labour income as capital income. It would also bring capital income taxes at the personal and the corporate level out of line. It would therefore have to involve a rather substantial reform of the entire tax system.

A tax on wealth is equivalent to taxing the normal (or risk-free) return to savings since it applies independent of the return that is achieved. As for example emphasised by the *Mirrlees Review* (2011), taxing the normal return is particularly harmful for saving and investment incentives since it in effect means taxing all types of assets, risk-free and risky, alike. Taxing above-normal returns would be distinctly less harmful as to a large degree it amounts to taxing the economic rents of risky assets, such as scarce resources or specialist knowledge, whose taxation causes little distortions. To capture the distortions through capital income and wealth taxes on saving and investment decisions, the primary focus should thus be on the ETR when assets earn the normal return. The nominal rate of return of 4% and the inflation rate of 2% assumed in Table 2.4 are close to the nominal rate of return to government bonds and consumer price inflation in Norway since 2000 and hence correspond to what is commonly used to proxy the normal rate of return. Table 2.A1.1 in Annex 2.A1 shows that in any case a similar pattern also emerges for variations in the choice of these values.

The wealth tax raises little revenue and potentially inhibits growth significantly

Given an ETR of more than 100% on a large part of interest-bearing accounts and shares in the economy, the wealth tax is likely to give rise to tax avoidance and evasion, although this is difficult to quantify. The revenue from the wealth tax is small; in 2010 it was NOK 12.6 billion which is equivalent to about 0.2% of all (recorded) household wealth or 0.8% of mainland GDP. To the extent that the wealth tax is not avoided and evaded, the very high ETRs that it implies penalise saving and investment and therefore potentially inhibit growth significantly. The Norwegian authorities should investigate the impact of the wealth tax on tax avoidance and evasion and incentives to save and invest. If the growth-equity trade-off is too unfavourable to growth, they should phase out or reduce the wealth tax.

Rather few countries in the OECD levy a wealth tax. In fact, only two, Luxembourg and Switzerland, raise more government revenue (as % of mainland GDP) with some form of wealth tax than Norway does (Figure 2.7). Sweden abolished its wealth tax in 2007, to avoid cumulative taxation of capital income and wealth, and because it suffered from exceptions that created loopholes and encouraged tax planning (Swedish Ministry of Finance, 2007). The wealth tax is controversial in Norway and has been much in the public debate. This controversy is reflected by the leader of the Confederation of Trade Unions (LO), the largest and most influential workers' organisation, calling on the government to re-evaluate the wealth tax, on the ground that it hinders investment (LO, 2011).

Phasing out the wealth tax would reduce the ETR on all assets (if imputed rents and capital gains on housing were taxed) to 56%, close to the top marginal tax rate on labour income of 54%. In the example above (see middle line in Figure 2.6) the total tax wedge after 30 years would be 75%. Phasing out or reducing the wealth tax might, however, be politically difficult because of its association with redistribution. A less complete reform should at least remove the undervaluation of real estate, business property and IPS pensions, while at the same time lowering the 1.1% statutory rate of the wealth tax. Raising the current threshold of NOK 750 000 would reduce the number of people paying the wealth tax but not solve the underlying problem of high marginal ETRs. To the extent that the government deems the progressive taxation of capital income desirable, an alternative to the wealth tax would be to add a surcharge to the 28% statutory tax rate on capital income above a certain amount (to reach, say, 35%). Compared to the wealth tax, this would on the one hand probably provide some unwelcome incentives for businesses to camouflage capital as labour income, on the other it would have the beneficial effect of increasing the transparency about the actual tax rates that apply to savings.

Figure 2.7. **Recurrent taxes on net wealth, 2010**[1]
As a percentage of GDP

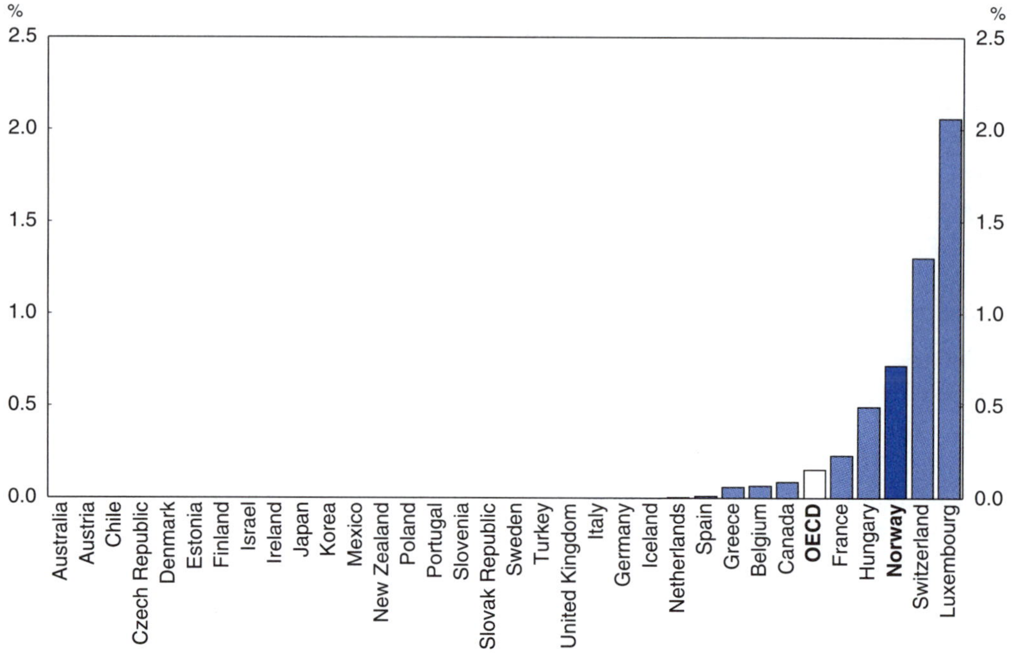

Note: Data for Norway refer to mainland. OECD area is the simple average of OECD countries for which data are available. The figures of GDP used for the calculations are those of the latest update available.
1. Or latest year available. Data refer to Revenue Statistics definition.
Source: OECD, *Revenue Statistics Database*.

StatLink http://dx.doi.org/10.1787/888932572444

On the face of it, phasing out or reducing the wealth tax appears to compromise the level of public revenue and the degree of redistribution which is likely to explain its popularity with some parts of the administration and the electorate. However, the actual revenue and redistribution effects might not be obvious. With no wealth tax, wealthy individuals may be induced to work more or hide less of their wealth abroad. This could lift revenues from personal (i.e. labour and capital) income taxation. Given the existing home bias in investment and the fact that most of the financial capital is owned by the 17% of the adult population who currently pay the wealth tax (see Figure 2.2), the implied rise in the post-tax rates of return could increase domestic investment. This might raise productivity, which should be reflected in higher wages and thus higher labour income tax revenues. For the same reason, part of the incidence of wealth taxes is probably borne by domestic workers whose wages are lower than they would otherwise be. Higher investment and growth would ultimately benefit households across the income spectrum.

Phasing out the wealth tax and introducing a personal allowance on capital income would help align effective capital with labour income tax rates

If the wealth tax were removed, the ETRs on most assets would be reduced to 56%, although this is still substantial, just above the top marginal tax rate on labour income but considerably higher than the lowest rate. To bring the ETR closer in line with labour income tax rates for small savers, the government could introduce a personal allowance for each citizen (say, of NOK 10 000 annually) on all capital income received. Variants of such an allowance are in place in several OECD countries, *e.g.* Germany. As stressed in the *Mirrlees Review* (2011), the allowance should, ideally, capture only the normal returns to investments. For shares, this would require excluding above-normal returns from the allowance and to refund the corporate income tax paid on the corporate level (up to the allowance).

From an efficiency perspective, such a personal allowance would help households to save part of their labour income for the future (*e.g.* to start a family, to start a business) as they might do without capital income taxes. From an equity perspective, an ETR of 0% (up to the allowance) would especially benefit poorer households for whom bank deposits (which currently attract an ETR of 56%) are likely the most important type of investment. The allowance would thus strengthen tax progressivity, counterbalancing potential effects from phasing out the wealth tax. If kept small, there should be few problems with people playing the system. There is, however, a risk that such an allowance would inflate over time due to lobbying activity and also set a precedent which might lead to public demands for less justified allowances elsewhere in the system.

To summarise, the government should aim at making the return to all asset classes subject to the same tax rate, without exemptions through undervaluations in the tax base, in particular those of owner-occupied housing.[6] The statutory tax rate on capital income should remain at 28% and a detailed analysis of the consequences of the wealth tax for avoidance and evasion behaviour and saving and investment incentives be undertaken. Phasing out or reducing the wealth tax could be combined with the introduction of a personal allowance on capital income which may make such a reform more easily feasible politically. The recommendations of an investigation into the wealth tax and introducing the taxation of imputed rents and capital gains from owner occupation are broadly in line with those of the Tax Committee (2003) which advocated abolishing the wealth tax and replacing it with a national property tax.

Gift and inheritance taxation

To a certain degree, wealth taxation indirectly taxes bequests prior to the occurrence of death. Phasing out or reducing the wealth tax may therefore decrease intergenerational mobility. This could affect the desired level of gift and inheritance taxation. Despite Norway's high level of overall tax revenue, revenue from gift and inheritance taxation is below the OECD average (Figure 2.8). The gift and inheritance tax falls on the recipient. Tax is due on gifts and inheritances a person receives during his lifetime from any other person above two thresholds: NOK 470 000 (level 1) and NOK 800 000 (level 2). These amounts apply per recipient and per donor. The rates differ between children[7] and other beneficiaries; they are 6% (level 1) and 10% (level 2) for children and 8% (level 1) and 15% (level 2) for other beneficiaries. In addition, each recipient has an annual allowance of currently NOK 39 608 in gifts and inheritances she receives from each other person. Gifts to persons other than children (as well as other persons who at the time of the donation are entitled to inherit the donor according to the inheritance law or the will of the donor) are tax-exempt. No tax on capital gains is triggered as a result of death. There are preferential rules for farms, non-listed shares and partnerships.

Current allowances and preferential rules should be replaced by a single lifetime allowance on all taxable gifts and inheritances

The current system of gift and inheritance taxation has a number of undesirable characteristics that undermine redistribution policy. Firstly, while gifts to a taxpayer's children are taxed, in order to avoid erosion of the inheritance tax base, gifts to others are untaxed. Hence, the tax system favours children at inheritance (by levying lower tax rates

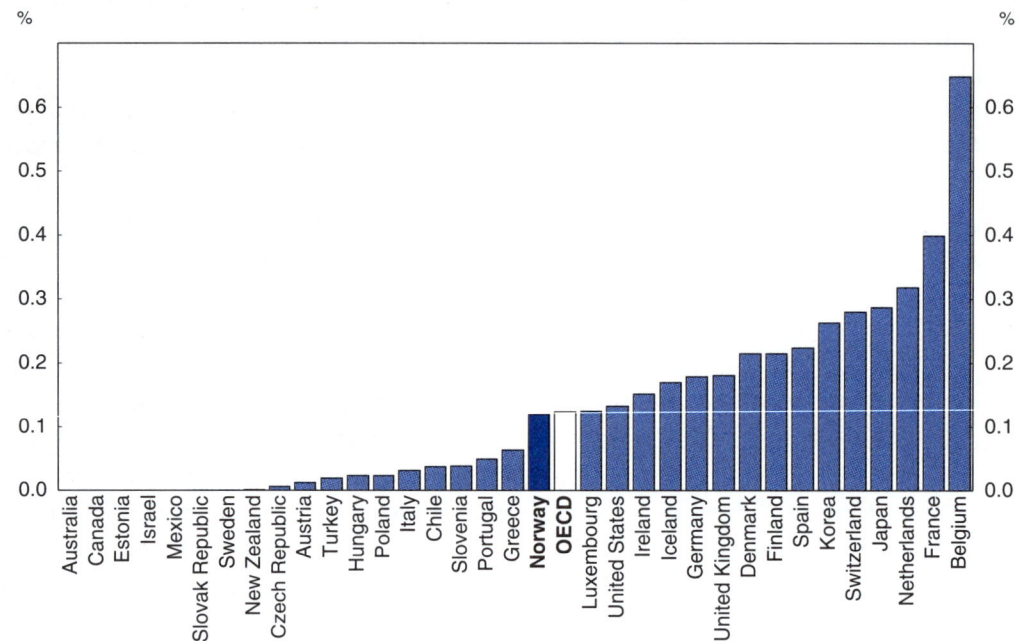

Figure 2.8. **Revenue from gift and inheritance taxation, 2010**[1]
As a percentage of GDP

Note: Data for Norway refer to mainland. OECD area is the simple average of OECD countries for which data are available. The figures of GDP used for the calculations are those of the latest update available.
1. Or latest year available.
Source: OECD, *Revenue Statistics Database*.

StatLink ⟶ http://dx.doi.org/10.1787/888932572463

on bequests to children) but discriminates against children for *inter vivos* transfers (by exempting gifts to other persons). Secondly, to the extent that gift and inheritance taxation is meant to promote equality of opportunity and intergenerational mobility, what should matter for the tax treatment of any additional gift or bequest is the total amount of gifts and bequests a recipient has already received during her life rather than from any particular person. The current design makes the gift and inheritance tax very obviously prone to tax avoidance behaviour, for example only taxing gifts to children invites the use of third persons to channel gifts to children. Thirdly, the annual allowance is likely to benefit especially the wealthier population which is better able to avoid the tax through careful tax planning. This is not so easy for households who have all their wealth tied up in a house, for example. Finally, exempting capital gains on bequests from taxation provides incentives for old individuals to hold on to their capital until death. The tax breaks on farms, non-listed shares and partnerships encourage keeping a business in the family, even if the economic arguments speak against it.

Important changes to the present system are therefore needed. Above all, these should see substituting current allowances and preferential rules by a single lifetime allowance. This single lifetime allowance should then apply per recipient and to the total amount of taxable gifts and inheritances she receives during her lifetime (and not for each donor separately). This implies no distinction is to be made between gifts and inheritances. Tax rates may continue to treat children somewhat preferentially over other beneficiaries, but this should be the same for gifts and inheritances. Capital gains of the donor upon the occurrence of death should be taxed, and the favourable rules applying to farms, non-listed shares and partnerships ought to be abolished.

Corporate income taxation

The taxation of businesses in Norway was subject to a tax reform in 2006 (for an evaluation, see Ministry of Finance, 2011b). The primary objective of the reform was to reduce the growing problem of income shifting; markedly higher statutory tax rates on labour income than capital income provided business owners with strong incentives to camouflage labour income as capital income. One important aim of the reform was also to ensure good general conditions for investing (and working) in Norway and that tax bases and resources were not lost to other countries.

The 2006 tax reform has successfully reduced income shifting by raising the tax rate on equity income and introducing an innovative rate of return allowance (RRA)

The taxation of equity income occurs in two stages, at the corporate level on corporate profits via the corporate income tax and at the personal level on dividends and capital gains via the personal income tax. The imputation system which was in place prior to 2006 granted a tax credit at the personal level for corporate income tax already paid. Since tax rates on corporate income and personal income were the same, it effectively exempted all dividends and capital gains from taxation at the personal level. The total statutory tax rate on equity income equalled the corporate income tax rate of 28%, which was significantly below the prevailing labour income tax rates. As such, the system provided businesses with strong incentives to shift labour income to capital income in their tax declarations.

The tax reform of 2006 introduced the innovative concept of a rate of return allowance (RRA). This maintained the tax exemption for equity income at the personal level up to the normal return; however, dividends and capital gains in excess of the normal return were subjected to an additional tax of 28%. Among all OECD countries, Norway has to date been the only one that has made use of an RRA. The economic rationale for the lower taxation of the normal return rests on the theoretical idea that a substantial part of above-normal returns accrues to economic rents (such as scarce resources or specialist knowledge). As emphasised *e.g.* in the *Mirrlees Review* (2011) or Sørensen (2005), above-normal returns should thus be taxed at a higher rate than normal returns which is precisely what is sought to be achieved with the RRA.

Since the reform, the combined statutory tax rate (corporate income tax rate plus personal income tax rate) on above-normal returns to equity income has been 48%. This is pretty much in line with current labour income tax rates. Table 2.5 shows the marginal labour income tax rates (including social security contributions) for self-employed individuals, small incorporated business owners and wage earners, separately for the lowest and highest labour income tax bracket. All rates are relatively close to the 48% statutory tax rate on capital income above the normal return, so that the incentives for misreporting the genuine type of income are contained. How large the benefits of the tax reform have been from the perspective of the income shifting problem depends on the scale of income shifting that was prevalent in the previous system, but little is known about this.

Table 2.5. **Marginal labour income tax rates**

	Lowest tax bracket (%)	Highest tax bracket (%)
Self-employed individuals:	39.0	51.0
Small incorporated business owners:	43.7	54.3
Wage earners:	43.7	54.3

Source: Ministry of Finance.

For large enterprises resident in Norway with ready access to the international capital market, the level and design of corporate income taxation will likely be the most important determinant within the tax system for the attractiveness of the location. Since this did not change, their conditions to invest should not have changed as a result of the reform. By contrast, for small and newly established companies relying on Norwegian equity, the provision of capital will, in addition to corporate income taxation, also depend on capital income taxation at the personal level. When below-normal returns are treated symmetrically to above-normal returns, the primary determinant of the distortions to investment through the tax system is the ETR on the normal return. In the absence of such symmetric treatment, the taxation of above-normal returns is likely to add to the distortions to investment as well. The tax reform of 2006 effectively increased the tax rates on dividends and capital gains above the normal return without providing for a fully symmetric treatment of below-normal and above-normal returns. This has weakened the neutrality properties of the RRA.

To limit the detrimental effects of capital taxation on investment, the RRA has the purpose of keeping the taxation of the normal return lower than it would otherwise be. However, the pure existence of the RRA in Norway does not mean that the normal return on equity income is in fact taxed less than above-normal returns. It merely means that the normal return is taxed less than it would be without the RRA. The normal return is usually approximated by the return to government bonds. Hence, as Table 2.4 shows, the taxation of purely inflationary gains implies that the (real) normal return to equity income is taxed at 56% for people not paying the wealth tax and 113% for people paying the wealth tax. Since above-normal returns are taxed at 48%, the normal return is in fact taxed more than above-normal returns, despite the RRA, whether or not a person is a wealth tax payer.

In some sense, it appears inconsistent to tax-exempt the normal return through the RRA and then tax the normal return through the wealth tax. However, in the absence of the RRA but with the same statutory rates, the ETR on the normal return to equity income would be even higher: about 100% for people not paying the wealth tax and 150% for people paying the wealth tax. A reasonably large fraction of the equity of Norwegian firms is financed by domestic sources. Removing the RRA would therefore significantly raise the funding costs of these firms, especially as a substantial part of the financial capital is likely to come from the 17% of the adult population paying the wealth tax (see Figure 2.2).

An allowance for corporate equity (ACE) would have been more suitable for attracting investment

An alternative to the RRA is an allowance for corporate equity (ACE), originally proposed by the Capital Taxes Group of the Institute for Fiscal Studies (1991). Table 2.6 summarises the key characteristics of the RRA and an ACE. Whereas the RRA taxes equity income at the statutory corporate income tax rate of 28% at the corporate level and exempts the normal return from taxation at the personal level, an ACE exempts the normal return from taxation at the corporate level and taxes equity income at the statutory capital income tax rate of 28% at the personal level. Put simply, the RRA effectively amounts to a

Table 2.6. **Statutory tax rates for a Norwegian resident investing in Norwegian equity**

	Rate of Return Allowance (RRA)	Allowance for Corporate Equity (ACE)
Corporate level:	Return fully taxed at 28%	Normal return tax-exempt Above-normal return taxed at 28%
Personal level:	Normal return tax-exempt Above-normal return taxed at 28%	Return fully taxed at 28%

reduction in the capital income tax rate at the personal level (relative to no allowance) and an ACE to a reduction in the corporate income tax rate (relative to no allowance). In a closed economy, the RRA and an ACE are equivalent.

This, however, is no longer the case in a relatively open economy like Norway. The RRA reduces the tax levy for Norwegian investors, even if they invest in companies abroad. By contrast, an ACE would reduce the tax levy on investments in Norway independent of the residence of investors. It is well-known that in a small open economy the corporate income taxes faced by international investors are likely a more important determinant of investment than the capital income taxes at the personal level faced by domestic investors. Accordingly, an ACE would have been more effective than the RRA in attracting more investment to Norway. Jacobsen (2008) uses the same arguments to make a similar point. Note as well that an ACE would have had the identical effects with respect to the primary objective (to prevent the tax-motivated shifting of income) as the RRA.

Is there a case for switching now from the RRA to an ACE? The answer depends mainly on the importance of attracting more investment to Norway. Two pieces of evidence may help. Mainland business investment as a share of mainland GDP lies at the lower end (Figure 2.9) and the level of the corporate income tax rate at the upper quarter of all OECD countries (Figure 2.10). While these factors raise some significant concerns about the attractiveness to invest in Norway, they do not on their own make a case for urgent reform of the RRA. Other changes to the tax system, such as removing the preferential treatment of housing or the very high ETRs for wealth tax payers, could be more important. However, corporate income taxes have been falling for a number of years across OECD countries. If this trend was to continue and re-initiate discussions about cuts in the corporate income tax rate in Norway, a shift from the RRA to an ACE seems to be a very attractive policy option. Contrary to cutting the corporate income tax rate, this would leave the other features of the tax system, notably the income-shifting problem, intact.

Using a switch from the RRA to an ACE to effectively cut the corporate income tax rate would also solve two problems in the current system: the non-symmetric treatment of

2. TAX REFORM IN NORWAY: A FOCUS ON CAPITAL TAXATION

Figure 2.9. **Non-oil business investment in international comparison**
As a percentage of GDP, 2010[1]

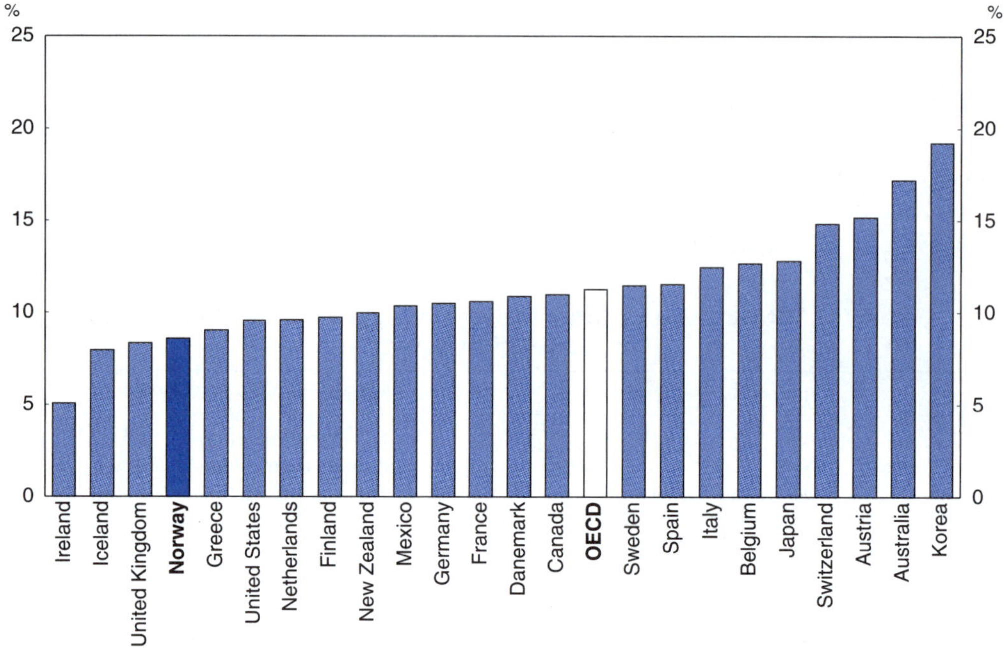

Note: Data for Norway refer to mainland. OECD area is the simple average of OECD countries for which data are available.
1. Or latest year available.
Source: OECD Economic Outlook Database.

StatLink ⟶ http://dx.doi.org/10.1787/888932572482

Figure 2.10. **Statutory corporate income tax rate,**[1] **2011**

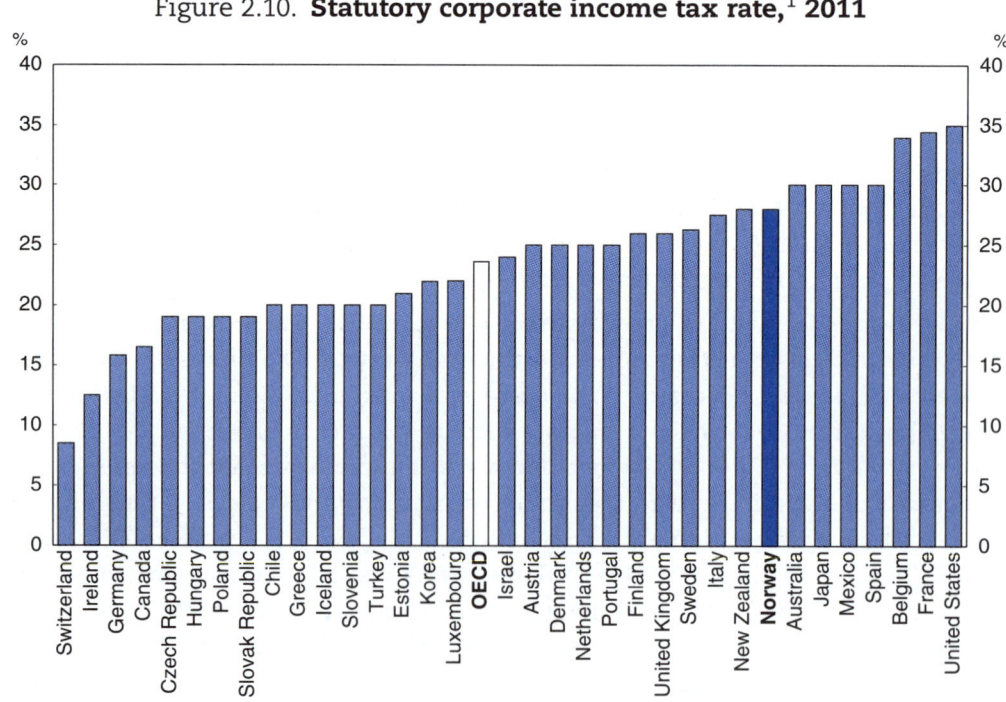

Note: OECD area is the simple average of OECD countries for which data are available.
1. Basic central government statutory (flat or top marginal) corporate income tax rate, measured gross of a deduction (if any) for sub-central tax.
Source: OECD Tax Database.

StatLink ⟶ http://dx.doi.org/10.1787/888932572501

below-normal and above-normal returns, and the non-neutrality between debt finance and equity finance. At the moment, the RRA is given to the investor owning the asset at the end of the calendar year, regardless of the actual time it has been in his possession. It would be practically impossible to keep track of the precise period of ownership for every taxpayer. This system, however, provides incentives to increase the portfolio of shares around New Year to increase the RRA. Such year-end trading is possible because some foreign investors are not entitled to the RRA. To counteract that, the investor loses any unutilised RRA at the time he sells the asset. The unwelcome consequence of this in turn is that the investor is no longer guaranteed a full offset of below-normal against above-normal returns. Similar problems would not arise with an ACE system where the allowance would be awarded when the tax on the corporate profits would be due.

The RRA achieves neutrality between debt finance and equity finance for a Norwegian investor (Table 2.7). For a foreign investor, however, while interest is deductible at the corporate level (which is of benefit to the foreign investor), the normal return to equity income is exempted from taxation only at the personal level (which is *not* of benefit to the foreign investor). The RRA fails to fix the discrimination of equity finance *versus* debt finance for foreign investors, thus providing multinational enterprises with incentives to undercapitalise their Norwegian subsidiaries. Replacing the RRA with an ACE would remove this anomaly, by ensuring that both the normal return to debt and the normal return to equity be exempted at the corporate level. This is one of the reasons why Griffith, Hines and Sørensen (2010) favour an ACE over the RRA.

Table 2.7. **Statutory tax rates on the normal return of investing in Norway**

	Rate of Return Allowance (RRA)		Allowance for Corporate Equity (ACE)	
	Debt	Equity	Debt	Equity
Norwegian investor:	28%	28%	28%	28%
Foreign investor:	Personal tax rate in home country	28% + personal tax rate in home country	Personal tax rate in home country	Personal tax rate in home country

The revenue impact of a switch from the current RRA to an ACE could go either way and would require model-based estimates. These would need to compare the "tax expenditure" through the RRA for Norwegian investors in domestic and foreign companies to the "tax expenditure" through an ACE for domestic and foreign companies locating in Norway. Importantly, they should account for the expected rise in business investment (and thus corporate income tax revenues) and productivity (and thus labour income tax revenues) in Norway that such a reform would entail. To limit the revenue loss through an ACE and prevent windfall gains to the owners of "old capital" already installed, the initial equity base should be zero for tax purposes, so that the ACE would be granted only for additions to the equity base undertaken after the time of the reform (Griffith, Hines and Sørensen, 2010).

To date, the two most important experiments with an ACE have been the profit tax in Croatia, which allowed a deduction for an imputed return on equity from 1994 to 2001, and the introduction of an ACE in Belgium in 2006. Keen and King (2002) argue that the Croatian ACE in many ways worked rather well. The experience with the Belgian ACE has been broadly positive from the point of implementation, although it also underscores the importance of careful design. For example, revenues from the corporate income tax shrank in the immediate years after the reform, partly because under pressure from lobbying the ACE was applied not only to new, as recommended in this *Survey*, but also existing equity.

One concern in many OECD countries are tax avoidance and evasion of capital income taxation (both at the corporate and the personal level) in a world of increasing international capital mobility. To promote effective worldwide co-operation in tax matters, the OECD has developed standards that have been endorsed by the more than 100 member jurisdictions of the Global Forum on Transparency and Exchange of Information for Tax Purposes. Norway has been an active member of the Global Forum since its creation. The peer review in OECD (2011b) documents that, notwithstanding some imperfections, Norway's practices with respect to exchange of information in tax matters are of very high standard.

Local property taxation

In 2010, 309 of the 430 municipalities exercised their right to levy a local tax on property at a rate between 0% and 0.7%. The local property tax raises very little revenue, representing only a tiny fraction of the entire revenue of all municipalities. If a municipality chooses to levy a property tax, it must decide whether to levy it: *i)* on all properties; *ii)* only on mills and factories; *iii)* only on all properties in urban areas; *iv)* only on mills and factories and all properties in urban areas; *v)* only on all commercial properties including mills and factories; or *vi)* only on all commercial properties including mills and factories and all properties in urban areas. Options *i)* and *ii)* are the most common among the municipalities that charge a local property tax (Table 2.8). No municipality has taken up option *iii)*, while options *v)* and *vi)* have only been introduced in 2011.

Table 2.8. **Use of the local property tax, 2010**

Municipalities charging no property tax:	121
Municipalities charging property tax:	309
All properties in the municipality	145
Mills and factories	129
All properties in urban areas	0
Mills, factories and all properties in urban areas	35

Source: Statistics Norway.

Revenues from local taxation to complement transfers from the national government are useful since they provide municipalities with some flexibility over the level and quality of the public services they are responsible for (Tiebout, 1956). Property values may indeed be a suitable tax base for such purposes, as they are, at least to a rough approximation, related to the consumption level of local public services, such as waste or cleaning. In other words, more expensive houses are typically bigger and hence produce more waste and require more street cleaning. Current revenue levels are consistent with this interpretation of the local property tax as a "benefit tax". They should certainly not be raised markedly if the other recommendations in this chapter to increase housing taxation – preferably through the introduction of the taxation of imputed rents and capital gains on owner-occupied housing at the national level – are followed through.

The central government should streamline the guidelines on local taxation of property and its valuation

At the moment, municipalities are free to decide among the six options to tax local property, and, theoretically, competition between them should encourage them to adopt the efficient choice. Realistically, this is unlikely, given limited mobility across municipalities and potential influence of political considerations on the design of the tax. Insofar as local property taxes represent benefit taxes, they should apply to all properties in the municipality in a similar way, since all properties in the municipality – both housing and business, in urban and rural areas – benefit from the public services financed with the revenue. In addition, to the extent that local property taxes are suitable to capture location-specific rents, they should indeed be set high. However, in such cases, corporate profits would seem the more appropriate tax base, an approach which is already used in the case of hydro power. Local property taxation could thus be improved by working towards the following reform of the national guidelines. Municipalities should continue to be able to set the local property tax at any level between 0% and 0.7% of the property values. The tax would, however, be due on all housing and business properties. In addition, extra charges may be applied to companies whose profits to a significant degree rely on location-specific rents.

Legislation requires the taxable values in the local property tax to reflect the market values. In reality, this is rarely the case. The taxable values are updated only every ten years, and municipalities frequently apply reductions that significantly reduce them below the market values. It is also common that differential rates are imposed on housing and commercial property. Except for extra charges that are clearly justified by location-specific rents, the national government should not provide municipalities with the freedom to grant any exemptions. These are only likely to cater to special interests and be inefficient.

In most municipalities, the property values used for the local property tax differ from those used for the wealth tax. Above, an investigation into the wealth tax was recommended. Should the wealth tax be retained, then the national government should strive to ensure that the same property values are used for both tax bases. This would almost certainly lead to lower administrative costs. In any case, a system should be put in place in which property values are updated at a higher frequency than now, say every three years.

The stamp duty on property transactions

A stamp duty of 2.5% of the market value of a property is due at the point it is legally transferred. The stamp duty must be regarded as a tax (not a fee) as it is not intended to cover the cost of the authorities for the registering of the acquired property. For this, a separate registration fee exists. The origin of stamp duties in most countries is that they are hard to avoid. In Norway, some property transactions are exempt from stamp duty, notably co-operatives. A co-operative is a contractual relationship that specifies that the property is jointly owned by all members and each member holds a "stake" in the co-operative proportional to the area of her flat.

To promote mobility, the stamp duty should be abolished

By increasing the costs of buying and selling houses, the stamp duty discourages people from moving to areas where their labour is in greatest demand (for empirical evidence, see *e.g.* Haurin and Gill, 2002; Van Ommeren and Van Leuvensteijn, 2005). Transaction taxes on house purchases have been shown to be an inefficient way of raising government revenue (OECD, 2009); the stamp duty should hence be discontinued. House prices are likely to have capitalised in the stamp duty; its abolition could therefore lead to an increase in house prices. In light of their currently high levels, the timing should thus be considered carefully. In any case, changes should be gradual to contain the windfall gains to current owners.

The economic consequences of the recommended reform measures

This final part of the chapter analyses the consequences of the recommended reform measures for economic growth, the public finances, the degree of redistribution through the tax system and the housing market.

The tax policy recommendations are conducive to enhanced economic growth and efficiency

Box 2.3 summarises the key tax policy recommendations. These should have beneficial effects for the allocation of capital and work and investment incentives, thereby promoting economic growth. As stressed in *Going for Growth* OECD (2011a), increasing the taxation of owner-occupied housing, preferably by taxing imputed rents and capital gains, would reduce the misallocation of capital that is likely present in the current system. Abolishing the stamp duty would promote residential and labour mobility. Phasing out or reducing the wealth tax would improve investment and work incentives, while eliminating loopholes in gift and inheritance taxation would facilitate intergenerational mobility.

... while their budgetary and redistributive implications could be broadly neutral

The proposed measures could be designed in a revenue-neutral way. An example of a possible reform package is illustrated in Table 2.9. The introduction of taxes on imputed rents and capital gains from owner-occupied housing and higher gift and inheritance taxation would increase tax revenue, whereas the newly proposed personal allowance on capital income and phasing out the wealth tax and stamp duty would have the opposite effect. The table presents estimates for the fiscal impact of three measures: the taxation of imputed rents and capital gains from owner occupation, phasing out the wealth tax and abolishing the stamp duty. Their sum is positive, indicating a surplus of NOK 23 (= 41 – 13 – 5) billion. This could be larger; the estimated budgetary gain from taxing owner-occupied housing is based on the historically low annual return of 3.3% and that from phasing out the wealth tax does not account for any behavioural effects, such as improved incentives to work and invest. Even with these conservative estimates, there would be enough fiscal room to set the personal allowance on capital income at a meaningful level, especially if the level of gift and inheritance taxes was increased. The precise budgetary implications of the personal allowance and gift and inheritance taxation would depend on the level of the allowance and the changes to the tax base and tax rates for gifts and inheritances.

From a political economy perspective, the progressive nature of the personal allowance on capital income and increased gift and inheritance taxation may be useful to garner political support for a phase-out of the wealth tax if all three measures were bundled in the same reform package. The example of a possible reform package is likely broadly neutral with respect to the degree of redistribution through the tax system (Table 2.9). Aligning the taxation of the returns to owner-occupied housing with rental housing would reduce inequality. The current system discriminates against less well-off citizens who are more likely to be tenants (and not home owners) and as a consequence bear a significant part of the burden of the tax their landlords must pay on rents. Similarly,

Table 2.9. **Budgetary and redistributive consequences of possible reform measures**

Possible reform measures	Budgetary consequences	Redistributive consequences
Introduce the taxation of owner-occupied housing	+ NOK 41 billion	+
Phase out the wealth tax	– NOK 13 billion	– –
Introduce a personal allowance on capital income	– ?	+
Increase gift and inheritance taxation	+ ?	+ +
Abolish the stamp duty	– NOK 5 billion	–

Note: Two signs in the right-hand column signal a strong effect.
Source: Ministry of Finance and OECD Secretariat.

a personal allowance on capital income and particularly higher gift and inheritance taxation would strengthen the progressivity of the tax system. The abolition of the stamp duty and phase-out of the wealth tax would benefit better-off households relatively more, although drawing this conclusion for the wealth tax abstracts from wage rises workers may receive as a result of increased productivity. The redistributive effects could be further strengthened by trading off a higher increase in gift and inheritance taxation with a more generous personal allowance.

Higher taxation of housing is likely to reduce household debt but also housing affordability

A key recommendation of this chapter is to tax owner-occupied housing like other asset classes, preferably through the taxation of imputed rents and capital gains from owner-occupied housing, which, even after phasing out the wealth tax, would likely lead to an increase in the taxation of housing. Would this help rein in house prices and hence household debt which, as shown in Figure 5, have experienced a significant increase over the last decade? A useful point of departure is that the housing cost approximates the present value of expected rents and the house price (as observed in the data) the housing cost minus the present value of expected tax liabilities. Accordingly, the short-run effect of a rise in the taxation of housing would be a drop in the house price, equal to the present value of expected increases in tax liabilities. The housing cost, however, would stay the same since the increased tax liabilities should to a large degree become capitalised in the house price.

With no other shocks to the economy, in the long run more capital would flow from housing to other forms of investment with higher pre-tax rates of return. This would raise the pre-tax returns (i.e. pre-tax rents) from housing investment and therefore lift the housing cost above the pre-reform level. With the housing cost rising, the house price would pick up accordingly. The higher housing cost would reduce the demand for housing; the house price would consequently stay somewhat below the pre-reform level. The implication is that the higher taxation of housing proposed in this chapter is likely to have a dampening effect on house prices and hence household debt, but it is also likely to increase the housing cost and thus decrease the affordability of housing. This is intuitive; increased taxation of housing is bound to make housing more expensive.

> **Box 2.3. Summary of recommendations on capital taxation**
>
> **Capital income taxation and wealth taxation:**
>
> - Align the taxation of different asset classes. This should include reducing the implicit tax subsidy to owner-occupied housing and removing the special treatment of real estate, business property and individual private (IPS) pensions in the wealth tax.
> - To tax owner-occupied housing like other asset classes, preferably imputed rents and capital gains from owner-occupied housing should be subject to the standard capital income tax rate of 28%. An alternative would be the introduction of a national tax on the market value of owner-occupied properties.
> - If neither imputed rent nor national property taxation is introduced, another possibility would be to remove mortgage interest deductibility. This would need to weigh up the benefits from higher effective taxation of owner-occupied property against abandoning the symmetric treatment of different sources of finance and interest that it would imply.
> - Investigate which persons participate in the tax-favoured individual private (IPS) pension scheme and the impact of the tax breaks on their total saving. If the results show that IPS pensions are primarily taken up by more well-off persons with no significant change to their saving, phase out all tax breaks to the scheme.
> - Effective tax rates through capital income and wealth taxes are very high. Investigate the impact of the wealth tax on tax avoidance and evasion and incentives to save and invest. If the growth-equity trade-off is too unfavourable to growth, phase out or reduce the wealth tax.
> - Phasing out the wealth tax would align effective tax rates on capital income with labour income tax rates of high income earners. If the wealth tax is phased out, consider introducing a personal allowance on capital income to bring effective tax rates on capital income closer in line with labour income tax rates also for low income earners.
>
> **Gift and inheritance taxation:**
>
> - Replace the current array of allowances, which facilitate tax avoidance by the wealthy, with a single lifetime allowance for all taxable gifts and inheritances from all donors.
> - Broaden the tax base by including *inter vivos* transfers to all types of beneficiaries and removing tax breaks to farms, non-listed shares and partnerships.
> - Tax capital gains on assets at the time of inheritance.
>
> **Corporate income taxation:**
>
> Should other countries continue to lower their corporate income tax rates, replace the current rate of return allowance (RRA) with an allowance for corporate equity (ACE).
>
> **Local property taxation:**
>
> - Harmonise the base of the local property tax across municipalities, so that all housing and business properties are included at full market valuation.
> - Update property values more frequently than currently, *e.g.* every three years. The same property values should be used for the local property tax as for the wealth tax.
>
> **Stamp duty:**
>
> Abolish the stamp duty on property transactions to promote mobility. Due to the possible effect on house prices, the timing should be considered carefully.

Notes

1. A range of other, often rather subtle, arguments exists. Firstly, in contrast to most costs in the production of income from financial capital, the costs in the production of income from human capital, *e.g.* foregone earnings, books, tuition, are not deductible. Therefore, by taxing capital income the government can provide an implicit subsidy to human capital investments to avoid individuals substituting financial for human savings (Jacobs and Bovenberg, 2010). Secondly, some individuals may accumulate precautionary savings to guard themselves against future (permanently) negative income shocks. Savings may then be taxed as otherwise those who prove able to maintain high labour incomes at a later stage in their life would have an excessively high incentive to work less (Golosov and Tsyvinski, 2006). Thirdly, capital market imperfections and uninsurable idiosyncratic shocks to the rates of return may justify shifting some inheritance taxation toward lifetime capital taxation (Piketty and Saez, 2011).
2. To be precise, the wealth tax in Norway is a *net* wealth tax as liabilities are subtracted from the tax base.
3. One example of a justified exemption from the neutrality across asset classes rule are some tax breaks to pensions which may induce people to save more for their retirement than they would otherwise do due to myopia.
4. Rental income below NOK 20 000 during a calendar year (which is a small amount) is tax-exempt, while if rental income is above this threshold the 28% tax rate applies to the full amount (also up to the NOK 20 000). The same rules apply when more than 50% of an owner-occupied property is rented out. Capital gains on owner-occupied housing are only taxable if the owner occupied the property for less than one of the two years prior to the sale.
5. This would not strictly speaking be sufficient due to the existence of a home savings (BSU) scheme which is meant to encourage young individuals (under age 34) to save for a future home purchase. It has a 20% tax deduction (to be claimed against ordinary income) for annual savings of up to NOK 20 000 in special accounts (with a NOK 150 000 limit on total savings).
6. The focus of this section is on aligning tax rates across asset classes on the normal return. To attain full symmetric treatment of assets, the government should, in principle, also strive to align tax rates across asset classes on above-normal returns.
7. The law treats parents who inherit from their children as equivalent to children.

Bibliography

Arnold, J.M., B. Brys, C. Heady, Å. Johansson, C. Schwellnus and L. Vartia (2011), "Tax Policy for Economic Recovery and Growth", *Economic Journal*, 121(550), pp. F59-F80.

Atkinson, A.B., and J.E. Stiglitz (1976), "The Design of Tax Structure: Direct *versus* Indirect Taxation", *Journal of Public Economics*, 6(1-2), pp. 55-75.

Attanasio, O., and M. Wakefield (2010), "The Effects on Consumption and Saving of Taxing Asset Returns", *Dimensions of Tax Design*, Oxford University Press, Oxford.

Banks, J., and P. Diamond (2010), "The Base for Direct Taxation", *Dimensions of Tax Design*, Oxford University Press, Oxford.

Boadway, R., E. Chamberlain and C. Emmerson (2010), "Taxation of Wealth and Wealth Transfers", *Dimensions of Tax Design*, Oxford University Press, Oxford.

Bond, S., and M.P. Devereux (1995), "On the Design of a Neutral Business Tax under Uncertainty", *Journal of Public Economics*, 58(1), pp. 57-71.

Brewer, M., E. Saez and A. Shephard (2010), "Means-Testing and Tax Rates on Earnings", *Dimensions of Tax Design*, Oxford University Press, Oxford.

Chamley, C. (1986), "Optimal Taxation of Capital Income in General Equilibrium with Infinite Lives", *Econometrica*, 54(3), pp. 607-622.

Devereux, M.P., and R. Griffith (2002), "Evaluating Tax Policy for Location Decisions", *International Tax and Public Finance*, 10(2), 107-126.

Diamond, P., and E. Saez (2011), "The Case for a Progressive Tax: From Basic Research to Policy Recommendations", *Journal of Economic Perspectives*, 25(4), pp. 165-190.

Golosov, M., and A. Tsyvinski (2006), "Designing Optimal Disability Insurance: A Case for Asset Testing", *Journal of Political Economy*, 114(2), pp. 257-279.

Griffith, R., J.R. Hines and P.B. Sørensen (2010), "International Capital Taxation", *Dimensions of Tax Design*, Oxford University Press, Oxford.

Haurin, D.R., and H.L. Gill (2002), "The Impact of Transaction Costs and the Expected Length of Stay on Homeownership", *Journal of Urban Economics*, 51(3), pp. 563-584.

Hines, J.R. (1999), "Lessons from Behavioral Responses to International Taxation", *National Tax Journal*, 52(2), 305-322.

Institute for Fiscal Studies (1991), *Equity for Companies: A Corporation Tax for the 1990s*, Institute for Fiscal Studies, London.

Jacobs, B. (2011), "From Optimal Tax Theory to Applied Tax Policy: Lessons from the Netherlands for Norway", mimeo, Erasmus University Rotterdam.

Jacobs, B., and A.L. Bovenberg (2010), "Human Capital and Optimal Positive Taxation of Capital Income", *International Tax and Public Finance*, 17(5), pp. 451-478.

Jacobsen, M.R. (2008), "Norwegian Economic National Report", in: *Yearbook for Nordic Tax Research 2008: Taxation of Capital and Wage Income; Towards Separated and or More Integrated Personal Systems*, DJØF Publishing, Copenhagen.

Joumard, I., M. Pisu and D. Bloch (2012), "Less Income Inequality and More Growth – Are They Compatible? Part 3: Income Redistribution via Taxes and Transfers across OECD Countries", *OECD Economics Department Working Paper*, No. 926, Paris.

Judd, K.L. (1985), "Redistributive Taxation in a Simple Perfect Foresight Model", *Journal of Public Economics*, 28(1), pp. 59-83.

Keen, M., and J. King (2002), "The Croatian Profit Tax: An ACE in Practice", *Fiscal Studies*, 23(3), pp. 401-418.

Kopczuk, W., "Economics of Estate Taxation: A Brief Review of Theory and Evidence", *Tax Law Review*, 63(1), pp. 139-157.

LO (2011), "LO and the Wealth Tax", Press Announcement, LO, Oslo.

Mankiw, N.G., M. Weinzierl and D. Yagan (2009), "Optimal Taxation in Theory and Practice", *Journal of Economic Perspectives*, 23(4), pp. 147-174.

Ministry of Finance (2011a), *The National Budget 2012*, Ministry of Finance, Oslo.

Ministry of Finance (2011b), *Report No. 11 to the Storting: Evaluation of the 2006 Tax Reform*, Ministry of Finance, Oslo.

Mirrlees Review (2011), *Tax by Design*, Oxford University Press, Oxford.

OECD (2009), *Economic Policy Reforms: Going for Growth 2009*, OECD Publishing, Paris.

OECD (2011a), *Economic Policy Reforms: Going for Growth 2011*, OECD Publishing, Paris.

OECD (2011b), *Global Forum on Transparency and Exchange of Information for Tax Purposes Peer Reviews: Norway 2011*, OECD Publishing, Paris.

Piketty, T., and E. Saez (2011), "A Theory of Optimal Capital Taxation", mimeo, Paris School of Economics and University of California at Berkeley.

Salanie, B. (2003), *The Economics of Taxation*, MIT Press, Cambridge, Massachusetts.

Södersten, J., and T. Lindhe (2011), "The Norwegian Shareholder Tax Reconsidered", *Department of Economics Working Paper*, No. 2011:6, Uppsala University.

Sørensen, P.B. (2005), "Neutral Taxation of Shareholder Income", *International Tax and Public Finance*, 12(6), pp. 777-801.

Swedish Ministry of Finance (2007), *Taxation of Capital and Wage Income; Towards Separated or More Integrated Personal Tax Systems*, Ministry of Finance, Stockholm.

Tax Committee (2003), *Press Release: Tax Committee Recommendations*, Ministry of Finance, Oslo.

Tiebout C.M. (1956), "A Pure Theory of Local Expenditures", *Journal of Political Economy*, 64(5), pp. 416-424.

Van Ommeren J., and M. Van Leuvensteijn (2005), "New Evidence of the Effect of Transaction Costs on Residential Mobility", *Journal of Regional Science*, 45(4), pp. 681-702.

ANNEX 2.A1

Effective tax rates on savings in different asset classes

The general formula for the effective tax rate (ETR) in Table 2.4, defined as the percentage reduction in the annual real rate of return on an extra NOK of saving caused by the tax system, is given by

$$\text{ETR} = \frac{(\text{pre tax real rate of return}) - (\text{post tax real rate of return})}{\text{pre tax real rate of return}}.$$

The pre-tax real rate of return r^{pre} is computed as

$$r^{pre} = \frac{1+i}{1+\pi} - 1,$$

where i denotes the nominal rate of return and π the inflation rate. It is convenient to decompose the nominal rate of return i on an asset additively into the normal rate of return i_N and the above-normal rate of return i_A, such that

$$i = i_N + i_A.$$

The post-tax real rate of return r_N^{post} on interest-bearing accounts, shares, owner-occupied housing and rental housing earning the normal return is computed as

$$r_N^{post} = \frac{[1 + i_N \cdot (1 - t_N)] - I(W > \overline{W}) \cdot 1.1\% \cdot v_W \cdot [1 + i_N \cdot (1 - t_N)]}{1 + \pi} - 1.$$

The indicator function $I(\cdot)$ equals 1 if the individual's tax-assessed wealth W exceeds $\overline{W}$ = NOK 750 000 and 0 otherwise. Hence, the second term in the numerator drops out for an individual not paying the wealth tax. Such an individual earns the normal rate of return i_N of which she can keep unity minus the statutory capital income tax rate t_N. This is 28% for interest-bearing accounts, shares and rental housing and 0% for owner-occupied housing (see Table 2.3).

An individual for whom $W > \overline{W}$ will in addition have to pay the wealth tax on the invested stock. The rate of the wealth tax is 1.1%, and v_W is the valuation of the asset class in the base of the wealth tax. This is 100% for interest-bearing accounts and shares, 25% for owner-occupied housing and 40% for rental housing (see Figure 2.5). Wealth tax payments are also assumed to be due on the nominal rate of return after the payment of the capital income tax.

Decomposing the post-tax real rate of return r^{post} on an asset earning above-normal returns into the post-tax real rate of return on the normal return and the post-tax real rate of return r_A^{post} on the above-normal return,

$$r^{post} = r_N^{post} + r_A^{post},$$

yields

$$r^{post} = r_N^{post} + \frac{i_A \cdot (1-t_A) - I(W > \overline{W}) \cdot 1.1\% \cdot v_W \cdot i_A \cdot (1-t_A)}{1+\pi}.$$

The rate of return allowance (RRA) implies that the statutory tax rate t_A = 48% on the above-normal return to shares is higher than the statutory tax rate t_N = 28% on the normal return. Since the RRA applies only to shares, for all other asset classes $t_A = t_N$.

The computation of the ETRs on individual private (IPS) pensions requires a number of additional assumptions which are spelled out in the note to Table 2.4.

This table displays the ETRs on the real income from different asset classes when the nominal rate of return is 4% and the inflation rate 2%. The choices for these variables correspond closely to the nominal rate of return to government bonds and consumer price inflation in Norway since 2000. As stressed in the *Mirrlees Review* (2011) and other sources, the primary determinant of distortions to saving and investment decisions through the tax system is the magnitude of the ETR on the normal rate of return. Table 2.4 therefore takes the return to government bonds, which is usually used to approximate the normal return, as the benchmark case.

The actual normal (or risk-free) rate of return (which is difficult to observe) may conceivably have a real rate of return that is less than 2%. Panel A in Table 2.A1.1 thus presents the ETRs on different asset classes for the case when the nominal rate of return is 3% (and the inflation rate continues to be 2%). Since the implied real return is now lower than with a nominal rate of return of 4%, while inflation is the same, the ETRs are higher than in Table 2.4.

Given full offset of below-normal against above-normal returns, the ETR on the normal return is the primary determinant of distortions to saving and investment decisions through the tax system even for risky assets demanding a risk premium (Bond and Devereux, 1995). However, the RRA does not treat below-normal returns fully symmetrically to above-normal returns. By implication, some investments would not be conducted even if only above-normal returns were taxed. The distortions to saving and investment decisions, when taking institutional limitations to a full offset of below-normal against above-normal returns as given, should then be gauged by an imputed rate of return which includes a risk premium (e.g. Griffith, Hines and Sørensen, 2010).

Panels B and C in Table 2.A1.1 assume a (nominal) normal rate of return of 4%, an inflation rate of 2% and a nominal rate of return of 5% and 6%, respectively. It is to be borne in mind that a real rate of return of 3-4% on interest-bearing accounts may not necessarily be plausible. Above-normal returns on shares incur an extra tax of 28%. Since this additional 28% tax on above-normal returns applies only to shares, the ETR on shares, with and without the wealth tax, rises relative to the ETRs on interest-bearing accounts, owner-occupied housing and rental housing, when compared to Table 2.4. Otherwise, a generally similar pattern emerges for these choices of values.

Table 2.A1.1. **Effective tax rates on the real income from different assets under alternative assumptions**

	Without wealth tax (%)	With wealth tax (%)
A. 3% nominal rate of return, 2% inflation rate		
Interest-bearing accounts	84	196
Shares	84	196
Owner-occupied housing	0	28
Rental housing	84	129
Individual private (IPS) pensions	73	73
B. 5% nominal rate of return, 2% inflation rate		
Interest-bearing accounts	47	85
Shares	53	91
Owner-occupied housing	0	9
Rental housing	47	62
Individual private (IPS) pensions	25	25
C. 6% nominal rate of return, 2% inflation rate		
Interest-bearing accounts	42	71
Shares	52	81
Owner-occupied housing	0	7
Rental housing	42	53
Individual private (IPS) pensions	20	20

Note: The calculations are done for a (nominal) normal rate of return of 3% in Panel A and 4% in Panels B and C. The effective tax rates (ETRs) apply to an extra NOK of saving by a Norwegian resident investing in a Norwegian asset. The ETRs for shares are based on nominal depreciation rates which are a reasonable approximation to how the Norwegian tax system functions as tax depreciation depends on the cost price (and not the repurchase price) and the expected life span of the asset. The ETRs for owner-occupied housing and rental housing are independent of the degree of debt finance *versus* equity finance when assuming that mortgage interest rates equal savings interest rates. The ETRs for IPS pensions are based on a tax rate on pension income of 39% and the assumption that the initial savings stay in the scheme for 15 years and are then paid out over a period of 15 years (as an annuity).
Source: Ministry of Finance.

ORGANISATION FOR ECONOMIC CO-OPERATION AND DEVELOPMENT

The OECD is a unique forum where governments work together to address the economic, social and environmental challenges of globalisation. The OECD is also at the forefront of efforts to understand and to help governments respond to new developments and concerns, such as corporate governance, the information economy and the challenges of an ageing population. The Organisation provides a setting where governments can compare policy experiences, seek answers to common problems, identify good practice and work to co-ordinate domestic and international policies.

The OECD member countries are: Australia, Austria, Belgium, Canada, Chile, the Czech Republic, Denmark, Estonia, Finland, France, Germany, Greece, Hungary, Iceland, Ireland, Israel, Italy, Japan, Korea, Luxembourg, Mexico, the Netherlands, New Zealand, Norway, Poland, Portugal, the Slovak Republic, Slovenia, Spain, Sweden, Switzerland, Turkey, the United Kingdom and the United States. The European Union takes part in the work of the OECD.

OECD Publishing disseminates widely the results of the Organisation's statistics gathering and research on economic, social and environmental issues, as well as the conventions, guidelines and standards agreed by its members.

OECD PUBLISHING, 2, rue André-Pascal, 75775 PARIS CEDEX 16
(10 2012 05 1 P) ISBN 978-92-64-12724-1 – No. 59803 2012-02